MORE DAVIDS
THAN
GOLIATHS

MORE DAVIDS
THAN
GOLIATHS

◆ ◆

A Political Education

◆ ◆

HAROLD FORD, JR.

Crown Publishers
New York

Copyright © 2010 by Harold Ford, Jr.

All rights reserved.
Published in the United States by Crown Publishers, an imprint of the
Crown Publishing Group, a division of Random House, Inc., New York.
www.crownpublishing.com

CROWN and the Crown colophon are registered trademarks of
Random House, Inc.

Library of Congress Cataloging-in-Publication Data

Ford, Harold, Jr., 1970–
More Davids than Goliaths : a political education / Harold Ford, Jr.—1st ed.
1. Ford, Harold, Jr., 1970–   2. Legislators—United States—Biography.
3. United States. Congress. House—Biography.   4. Tennessee—Biography.
I. Title.
E840.8.F665A3 2010
328.73'092—dc22
[B]   2010005486

ISBN 978-0-307-40838-9

Printed in the United States of America

Design by Lauren Dong

10 9 8 7 6 5 4 3 2 1

First Edition

To the voters of the Ninth Congressional District of Tennessee for giving life to my dream, and to Emily, who enriches life every day

Contents

MORE DAVIDS
THAN
GOLIATHS

The APPRENTICE

THIS IS HAROLD FORD, JR., AND I'M CAMPAIGNING for my daddy for Congress. If you want a better house to live in, better schools to go to, and lower cookie prices, vote for my daddy." I made my first political ad when I was four years old. It was 1974, and my father was running for Congress. My mom propped me up on a brown folding table at the back of my dad's campaign headquarters and I spoke into a microphone attached to a cassette recorder.

I did it in one take.

Politics was ingrained in me early. It was part of me in the best of ways. For my entire life, I've met and heard people, especially other politicians, talk about how they started early in politics by handing out leaflets, brochures, and so on. My start in politics was equally honest—a commercial for my dad on his first congressional campaign. In a lot of ways, politics was—and remains—a part of my genetic makeup, and, for that matter, so was my party identification. I learned to be a Democrat the old-fashioned way: I was told that I was going to be one by my father and mother.

◆   ◆

The campaign headquarters was a comfortable setting for me. I was there almost every day. My folks would pick me up at preschool and take me to the headquarters, where I delighted in the hustle and bustle and the steady inrush and outrush of staff and volunteers. For as long as I can remember, I've loved being around people.

As a kid, I always felt comfortable around adults. I didn't necessarily prefer adults over my peers, but sitting with, listening to, and talking in front of adults never really bothered me or made me nervous. I wasn't overconfident or anything like that. But I wasn't lacking confidence—I get that from both my mom and my dad. Nor was I different from other kids my age in that I enjoyed and played sports. It was more that I wanted to be a part of the conversation—I wanted to help in any way I could. I felt a particular but unarticulated closeness to the politics surrounding me—perhaps because it was my family involved and my dad's name on the ballot.

A few days after I made the ad, I heard it on the radio. I was sitting between my parents in the car. My mother smiled. My father grinned. I remember, at a precocious moment, thinking at the time, "I enjoy talking, and I really enjoy talking about campaigning." Although I didn't appreciate what exactly my dad was going to do to get people better homes and kids better schools, I knew he was going to try.

◆   ◆

AFTER THE AD, I started going to more and more campaign events with my parents. It isn't uncommon for politicians to introduce their families or even to ask their families to join them onstage while they are speaking. And my dad would often do that. He would sometimes allow me to introduce him, and I often repeated my line from the radio ad. The cookie line was my favorite line in the introduction—my mother drafted that line.

When introducing my dad, I always committed the additional lines to memory. I never used notes or read from a prepared text—even to this day, I don't use prepared remarks. I will sometimes refer to notes, but never a written speech. I don't use prepared remarks primarily because I find them hard to read with passion, sincerity, and force.

I remember speaking at one of my father's congressional prayer breakfasts in Memphis when I was seven. My dad's speaker that year was his congressional colleague and my parents' longtime friend Andrew Young. I helped introduce Congressman Young. I reminded the audience how much a role model Congressman Young was to people of all ages, especially for aspiring politicians like me. Prior to the speech, I remember going with my dad and some other politicians to meet with Congressman Young in his hotel in downtown Memphis. I sat at the dining room table in the hotel with Congressman Young and my dad as they discussed politics. I was just absorbing. My dad's focus was always people, especially hardworking poor people. My dad was listening closely to Congressman Young talk about how he and Maynard Jackson

had built a black-white coalition in Atlanta premised on pro-
pelling black elected officials into high political offices and
growing business opportunities for the entire Atlanta business
community, including minority businesses. Memphis's persis-
tent and pernicious occupation with race had prevented us
from electing an African American mayor and widening sus-
tainable business opportunities and growth to black businesses
in the city. My dad's belief was that a racially diverse and successful Memphis business community was essential to better
political and social cohesion in Memphis. One of the keys to
realizing that dream was for the Memphis political landscape
to become more racially and politically diverse first. Atlanta
was a model for Memphis.

One of the things I learned from my dad at an early age
about politics was never to allow jealousy, envy, or pettiness to
get in the way of learning from a political peer. My dad inspired and taught a lot of politicians, younger and older, but he
never shied away from learning himself. Andrew Young and
Maynard Jackson are two southern politicians whom my dad
respected and learned from.

Growing up in a political household seemed normal because it's all I knew. There were three basic givens in the house
for Jake, Isaac, and me. We had to do our homework every
night, we had to go to church every Sunday (and oftentimes
Sunday school), and we worked on political campaigns for my
dad and my uncles.

There was only one of those I genuinely enjoyed and relished—campaigning. Don't get me wrong, my parents didn't
force us to campaign, but it was expected. And my brothers

When my parents were attending political and social events in the evenings, they would leave my brothers and me with one of the most wonderful families I've ever known, the Ingrams. The Ingram girls, Lori and Debra, were our primary babysitters. Their mother, Mrs. Ingram, was the moral pillar of the household, and she insisted that everyone accompany her to Lambert Church of God in Christ on Wednesday nights. We knew that if we went to the Ingrams' on a Wednesday night, we would be going to church. It didn't occur to us to argue. Wednesday night church wasn't ideal, since we had just gone to church three days earlier and were due again in church four days later. However, Wednesday night church was bearable because the choir sang well at Lambert, and the pastor's sermon was not as long on Wednesday as it was on Sunday. Although, Church of God in Christ sermons were always longer.

On Sunday, the thought of after-church dinner eased some of the pain of sitting through services.

The Ford family convened for Sunday dinner at my dad's parents' home on Golf Club Circle. Newton Jackson, or "N.J." as everyone called him, and Vera Ford—we called her Grandma Vera—were the patriarch and matriarch of this sprawling Ford family. N.J. and Vera had fifteen children between them, and twelve had survived—eight boys and four girls. I had so many cousins that I sometimes lost track. Every Sunday meal felt like a family reunion. During election season, there were always politicians joining us for dinner—some elected and others aspiring. Anyone running for governor, senator—even president with Jimmy Carter—made his or her way to South Memphis to have dinner at my grandparents' home after church. It wasn't uncommon for forty to be seated for dinner on a Sunday evening.

My grandfather was always there to greet us when we arrived, still in our church suits and clip-on ties. A regal man with soft gray hair, he'd say, "Come to Granddaddy," and reach into his pocket for a dollar's worth of quarters. On any given Sunday, there were a dozen or more kids running around the house; during the holidays, there were more. My grandfather spent much of the evening surrounded by jostling groups of grandkids.

My grandmother and aunt Joyce—and sometimes my mother, who is quite a cook herself—handled the cooking responsibilities. They cooked huge, delicious dinners: turkey, fried chicken, spaghetti, sweet potatoes, string beans, collard greens, squash, cabbage, candied yams (still my favorite—thankfully, my wife and mother-in-law make them for me now), sliced tomatoes, dressing, rolls, and corn bread. It wasn't the best dinner if one was trying to diet, but it was some kind of good.

N.J. sat at the head of the table and led the conversations. He would tuck his big white cloth napkin into his collar to keep sweet potatoes and collard greens off his shirt and tie. He said grace only after Vera sat down next to him and received his thanks for preparing the meal. It didn't matter how powerful the politicians at the table were; they all waited for my grandmother. My grandfather stood before she took her seat. When politicians and candidates came to N.J.'s home for Sunday dinners, he grilled, dazzled, and charmed them all at once. N.J.'s influence was local, but his political interests were broader than Memphis and Tennessee. His involvement and leadership in the national association of black funeral directors provided him a large and substantive business platform to discuss politics. My grandfather didn't hesitate to ask politicians about their families and personal lives while also measuring their political beliefs and agendas against his own.

I sat at the kids' table in the kitchen along with my brothers and a dozen or so cousins. (When I was elected to Congress, I finally got to sit at the adults' table.) When we finished eating, long before the adults, we would pile into a guest bedroom in the house and watch *Hee Haw*, a Southern favorite. I loved spending time with my cousins. My uncles Joe and John and my aunts Ophelia and Joyce came to dinner with their children almost every Sunday. Aunt Joyce's daughters, Bilene, Pam, Vicki, and Jeannie, and Aunt Ophelia's daughter, Sophia, were like sisters to my brothers and me. My father's older siblings lived in New York and California, and they came with their kids on holidays and during the summer. Smart and sophisticated, my out-of-town cousins were great role models for the younger cousins. I remember when my cousin Lewis accepted a football scholarship to Stanford. My cousin Teresa graduated from Harvard Business School, and another cousin, Debbie, graduated from Harvard Law School. Debbie's sister, Shelly, graduated from Columbia School of Journalism. It was the first time I'd heard of these schools. Most of my dad's family, including my dad, were graduates of Tennessee State University in Nashville, a prestigious and historically black school. My father's educational journey continued at mortuary school in Nashville and later at Howard University's School of

Business. My dad entered Howard's program shortly after we moved to Washington in 1979. It was clear to me that my mother wanted her boys to follow the college paths of their out-of-town cousins.

IN DECEMBER 1863, two slaves named Jackson and Essex Geeter escaped from a Mississippi plantation. The men were brothers. They made their way to a Union Army camp in La Grange, Tennessee, where they enlisted. For the next two years, they served with distinction; Essex rose to the rank of corporal. After being honorably discharged in 1866, they settled in southwest Shelby County—now South Memphis—and bought property. By the time Essex decided to run for a seat on the county school board many years later, he had become a widely respected member of the community. He won the seat and initiated my family's tradition of public service.

Essex's brother Jackson also prospered. When he passed away in the summer of 1920, his widow, Sallie Geeter, deeded land to Shelby County for the establishment of an elementary school. Geeter School, which still stands, has educated thousands of kids from South Memphis, including my father and his siblings.

Albert Ford, another former slave some years older than Essex and Jackson, settled near the Geeters in Shelby County. Albert's son, Newton F. Ford, ran for a seat on the Shelby County Court at the same time Essex Geeter ran for a seat on the county school board. On August 2, 1888, they both won their races.

The Geeter and Ford families were formally united when Newton's son, Lewie C. Ford, married Ophelia Edna Geeter, daughter of Jackson and Sallie Geeter. Ophelia gave birth to my grandfather, Newton Jackson Ford (N.J.).

N.J. carried on the family tradition of public service. Although he lost a bid for the Tennessee state legislature in 1965, he was elected as a delegate to the Tennessee Constitutional Convention in 1977. It was an influential position in Tennessee politics. N.J.'s public service wasn't limited to running for and serving in public office. He helped fund children's education and sports programs and was an active supporter of the Boy Scouts of America. He was a lifetime member of the NAACP. As the founder and owner of a successful funeral home in South Memphis, he considered it his duty to give back to the community. I remember looking through photo albums dedicated to N.J.'s philanthropic work; in many of the photos, he was being honored for his contributions to local causes and organizations.

Although my grandmother Vera Ford never ran for or was appointed to any office, she was a dynamic political force. She was voted Tennessee Mother of the Year and continually honored by the state for her service to her community.

NOVEMBER 4, 1974, was a historic night for the Ford family. My father won his congressional seat, and two of my uncles, John and Emmitt, prevailed in their respective races for state senate and state house. It was the first time in American history that three brothers had been on the same ballot on the same day and all won.

My father became the first African American elected to Congress from Tennessee. He was the first—and is still the only—African American Democrat to unseat an incumbent Republican congressman, and he won despite the fact that the federal government had not required Tennessee to redraw congressional districts after the 1970 census to guarantee minority representation. The district was predominantly white.

Fortunately for my father, his opponent, Dan Kuykendall, had lost touch with the voters. Although Kuykendall had been in office for several terms, he fell victim to a strong anti-Republican political current fueled by Watergate and a young, dynamic, tireless, and fearless challenger—my dad.

Presumably to deny my father both publicity and equal status, Kuykendall refused to debate him throughout the campaign. Kuykendall believed that sharing a platform with Harold Ford was beneath him. He never imagined that a state representative with a big afro from South Memphis could beat him.

My father was undaunted. He campaigned and campaigned. He accepted every invitation he received to attend candidate forums and debates, even when Kuykendall refused to show. When Kuykendall was a no-show to debates, my father would bring a briefcase and place it in front of the chair or podium where Kuykendall was supposed to sit or stand. After my father finished answering a question, he would look at the stand-in briefcase and proceed to give Kuykendall's answer, which he derived from Kuykendall's voting record. So, when the questions in a debate turned to health care, he pulled out several documents proving Kuykendall's slavish support of the pharmaceutical industry over the needs of senior citizens and working people.

My dad outworked and outcampaigned Kuykendall. He had no choice because history and demographics were not on his side. On Election Day, my dad and his team gathered in their war room. To count votes, he largely relied on two people, Osbie Howard and Frank Banks. They remain great friends today. I don't remember much about that campaign, but I'll never forget Osbie and Frank constantly putting up numbers on a Memphis precinct map in the war room. My dad had a volunteer or a staffer at every polling place in the district, and as soon as the polls closed and the votes were counted, the staffer or volunteer would collect the numbers off the voting machines and call. (The actual ballots were then physically transported to the Elections Commission office for certification.)

The counting was slow, but my dad, Frank, and Osbie had built a prediction model based on turnout and win-loss margin in specific precincts. Early on, it became clear that my dad was overperforming in his base areas. The trend continued, and finally, late that night, Frank and Osbie said, "Harold, we think you've won it. We think you won this race by fewer than 500 votes."

Not long after Frank and Osbie's declaration, the local media began reporting that my dad was losing decisively, by nearly 5,000 votes. News of an impending Kuykendall victory was spreading. Kuykendall started doing interviews suggesting that he had won.

Frank and Osbie saw the media reports. My dad insisted that they recheck their numbers. "There's no way. That's not plausible. Unless we're missing something and our numbers are completely off." So they did the math again. They reached the same conclusion: My dad had won by roughly 500 votes. The local news declared Kuykendall the winner based on the final results from the Elections Commission. My father decided that the only way to reconcile Frank and Osbie's numbers—and his own belief that he had won—with the Elections Commission's final numbers was to go down to the Elections Commission headquarters and demand a recount.

What happened then transformed politics in Memphis and introduced the city and the region to a new era of public service.

"I have reason to believe these numbers are not accurate," my dad said at the commission, "and I want to contest them." He was told flatly that the race was over, he had lost, and he would get no recount. When he argued, he was met with racial epithets. "You niggers go home," someone said. "You lost."

The ballots, it turned out, were still being transported and unloaded in a garage behind the building. A cleaning woman on swing shift, who happened to be passing by, told my father about the tremendous activity in the garage. My dad walked over to the area where the cleaning lady had been and began poking around, inspecting trucks and ballot boxes. He soon noticed several stacks of sealed boxes and realized that the boxes contained ballots from several of the largest black precincts in the city. My dad was unsure of the status of the ballots. Meaning, he couldn't verify if they had been counted yet and were a part of the final tally. He was suspicious because the boxes containing the ballots were sealed. After a few minutes of not being able to get a credible answer from anyone in the garage about the ballots, my dad was convinced—the Memphis political power structure was trying to steal the election from him.

"We've done the math ourselves very carefully," he said, "based on official tallies from the precincts, and here we are being told that we've lost and can't get a recount—yet we've got sealed boxes of ballots sitting here at the Elections Commission. We're not going home until those ballots are counted," my dad told the press.

It wasn't long before the election commissioners appeared and publicly conceded that my father had won. They declared him the victor before they had even counted all the ballots in question.

Kuykendall was on a local TV news show declaring his victory when he was passed a note saying that in fact my dad had won the race. He walked off the air without a word. He never bothered to congratulate his opponent.

The commissioners were never held accountable for attempting to steal the race. No one was indicted and no one was reprimanded for any infraction or violation. They claimed that they had simply overlooked a few boxes of ballots. No serious mistakes, they said, had been made.

In the end, my dad won by a margin of 532 votes. Frank and Osbie had been off by 32 votes.

◆   ◆

FROM THE BEGINNING, campaigning was a part of my existence. I enjoyed everything about it. I loved being surrounded by people. I loved speaking at events. I would walk around the house imitating my dad and his speaking style. I'm blessed in many ways, and one of them is that I've never been real nervous when speaking publicly.

During campaign season, my father rose early to visit busy breakfast spots. He would spend afternoons and evenings catching up with people in grocery store parking lots and shopping centers. During rush hour, he stood at busy intersections, walked through neighborhoods, knocked on doors, distributed literature, and put up campaign signs. He believed absolutely in the power of touching and meeting people where they worked, shopped, lived, and worshipped. He campaigned like this every cycle. Retail politics was where you learned the voters' concerns and aspirations. This kind of human connection was the soul and most important principle of his politics—and it became mine, too.

"You have to touch people three times," he told me. "They have to meet you and come away from that initial encounter with positive feelings about you. Then they have to see you in a setting they're comfortable in, and realize that you're comfortable in that setting as well. And finally, they have to see you speaking convincingly and passionately about something they care about. And then you have to deliver for them," he would say.

At eight, ten, and twelve years old, I watched my dad interact with people and take mental notes of every encounter. His mental note-taking led to action. He would get back to the car or the office and dictate to someone what he had learned and the recommended course of action. He would often look at his staff and say, "Follow-up is the most important thing to constituent service." He was right.

I remember my father taking me to our small local barbershop in South Memphis when I was four. The barbershop was called Rosewood. The aptly nicknamed owner and lead barber, Slim, was slender and tall. There was a lot of talk about sports, current events, politics, and pop culture. Slim had political posters, pictures, and framed news articles on the wall, along with what looked to be framed album covers from the '70s R & B/funk band the Ohio Players. The women adorning the album covers inspired everyone in the barbershop. There were also *Jet* and *Ebony* magazines on side tables.

People in the barbershop asked my dad for help with every imaginable issue and challenge—from paying a bill to getting a loan to finding their relative or neighbor a job. My father was so accustomed to hearing how the local power company mistreated poor and working people with punishing late fees that he launched a crusade against the public utilities to force them to alter their billing practices and ultimately the gender and racial composition of the workforce and board. He helped do the same with the local police and fire departments as well. This effort was the result of listening to security guards at buildings, nurses at hospitals, cashiers at car washes and movie theaters, mechanics at service stations, and housekeepers waiting for the bus.

Everywhere my dad went, he introduced himself and asked for people's votes. After a few terms, he was well-known for his effectiveness, but he never assumed that people knew who he was or that he had their support. That puzzled me. They did know who he was, and he enjoyed overwhelming support. I finally asked him about it.

"Harold," he said, "never take a vote for granted. I don't care if you're talking to your best friend. Ask for his vote." And he told me the infamous political story: After losing a race badly, a politician went to his next-door neighbor's house and asked why the neighbor hadn't voted for him. "You never asked," the man said.

By the time I turned seven, I was approaching people myself, extending my hand, and saying, "I'm Harold Ford, Jr., and I want you to vote for my dad for Congress."

To draw people out into the streets, my father used to rent buses and band floats and drive through communities with a band on the float. We would pass out ice cream to kids and waving fans to their parents and grandparents. The fans all read "Vote for Harold Ford." We went right to where people lived. Every activity my father engaged in and every gesture he made was designed to accentuate a personal touch.

Retail campaigning was my introduction to politics. It was the nucleus of everything political, and I equated it with constituent service; during campaigns, my dad promised voters that he would take care of their needs once elected. And he did. It was critical to walk through neighborhoods and senior centers and barbershops, through beauty shops and grocery and department stores, in order to see and hear people's concerns.

◆   ◆

Constituent service was the backbone of my father's political work. Casework was the most important job in his office. Everyone who worked for him had two titles, one automatically being "caseworker." Resolving constituents' problems, no matter how seemingly small, was the most significant work anyone in the office could do. My dad determined whom he hired based on how serious they were about constituent service. Everyone who came in looking for a job was told, bluntly, "What we focus on here is casework."

When a constituent called, my dad's staff was expected to get to work on the problem immediately, regardless of its nature. Writing a letter to a state or federal agency was insufficient. Staffers had to both write a letter and make the call and then send a copy of the letter to the constituent. They would be judged not just by how many calls they took and how many people they called back, but also by how many cases they resolved. In my dad's office, there was no victory dance when a staffer closed out a case. It was what was expected, not by my dad but by the people they worked for—the constituents.

My father had refined the process so that problems got resolved in the most efficient way possible—firmness and persistence were encouraged.

No staffer ever graduated from casework, and my dad never stopped doing it himself.

After school, I would often visit my dad's district office and watch his staffers work through constituent problems. The more time I spent there, the more I wanted to do it myself.

Many of the calls my father fielded had little to no connection to the federal government. People wanted help with apartment repairs, bill payment extensions, and other concerns we heard expressed at the barbershops and beauty shops.

I was seven years old when I started answering phones and routing calls to caseworkers. The office protocol required the gathering of pertinent information. After answering, "Congressman Harold Ford's office; can I help you?" I would attempt to elicit the constituent's information and then pass it on to a caseworker.

The more I did it, the more I came to understand how cases got resolved—which agencies to call, which follow-up questions to ask, and so forth. If a caseworker was talking to a landlord who had illegally raised a constituent's rent, for example, the caseworker needed to know the average rent for apartments of that size. If someone had been charged an exorbitant late fee, a caseworker needed to take a look at the rental agreement.

I remember listening to a caseworker deal with a rental late fee. A woman had been charged a late fee that amounted to 30 percent of her rent. Upon hearing from one of my dad's caseworkers, the property manager immediately offered to lower the fee. The caseworker said, "No, sir. I don't want you to lower it in this one case just because I called. I want you to lower it for everyone else in your building for every time you raised it." And he did.

◆   ◆

MY INVOLVEMENT IN casework got personal one summer day when I was nine years old. I had gone to the office with my dad. The office was particularly crowded—lots of walk-ins that day.

I noticed that one overwhelmed caseworker was having trouble getting back to a constituent. I told the caseworker that I knew about the case—it was a Social Security issue, and I had listened to him work on it and read the case file—and asked if he wanted me to call the constituent back with a status report. He said he would appreciate it and seemed grateful, so I called the constituent back. It went well.

From then on, if an issue wasn't too complicated, my dad's staffers would ask me to call constituents back and give status reports.

I'd say, "The caseworker said he will call you back this afternoon. But rest assured that what you talked about is being resolved."

"Oh, thank you. Thank you."

Once, I took a call from a woman who needed a repair done in her apartment. She had been calling her landlord for weeks, but to no avail. I was confident I could handle the case.

"You think you can drive out here and see how bad things are?" she asked, not knowing I was nine. She was greatly distressed. "Can you please come out and look into it?"

I didn't have the heart to tell her that I didn't have a driver's license.

"I'm going to call the landlord right now and figure out why he hasn't responded," I said, "and we'll get somebody out there if we can't get it resolved."

I took down all her information and then called her landlord. He wasn't in, so I left a message.

When he called back an hour later, I was still in my dad's office. My dad was at lunch, and I'd gone into his office to sit at his desk, which I liked to do whenever I could. My dad often talked on the phone while reclining deeply in his chair, his feet up on the credenza. I always imitated him when he wasn't there, and when the landlord's call came through, I was sitting behind the desk, leaning back in the chair as far as I could, with my feet up on the credenza.

Nobody ever called me in the office directly but my mom and dad, so I knew it had to be either the constituent or her landlord. I picked up the phone. It was the landlord.

"I was calling regarding the situation you phoned about," the landlord said.

"Yes," I said, with a hint of nervousness, "this is Harold Ford, and I was calling to talk about the situation. It appears that you've taken a long time to get to this repair."

"Yeah?" he said.

"Well, she called us and she's saying she's having trouble getting you to repair it. Do you have any idea when you might be able to get it done?"

"We're getting on it."

"Can you tell me when the call was made from her to you asking for it to be repaired?"

He paused for a second and said, "I don't remember. Pretty recently."

"Well," I said, "I don't believe you. I would be happy to come over and sit with you to figure out how we can get this done a little more quickly," I said anxiously, because there was no way I could drive over there.

"Look, I told you we're going to get this done. It's taken us a while to get to it, but it's going to get done," the landlord said with rising irritation.

"She said this was the third time she'd called, and the repair normally takes a short period of time. It's inconveniencing her and her kids. So if there is any way I can be helpful—"

"Let me ask you a question," he interrupted. At this point, I turned around and took my feet off the credenza.

"How old are you?" he asked.

I paused—should I lie or tell the truth? "I'm nine."

"Is this Harold Ford's office?"

"Yes. I'm Harold Ford, Jr."

He hung up the phone.

I distinctly remember the feeling of being dismissed. I was mad. And fired up even more to help the constituent. I felt a stronger connection to the constituent, and it motivated me to find someone in the office to solve the constituent's problem. I immediately gave the constituent's information to a senior caseworker, and he called the landlord back and resolved the situation.

When my dad returned from lunch, the caseworker told him what had gone on, and they laughed about it. The caseworker said, "Your son called this landlord, and the guy couldn't believe he was talking to a nine-year-old. When he realized it, he just refused to respond to Harold Jr. But your son wouldn't let up."

"That's Harold Jr.," my dad told his staffer.

Later, at home, my dad told me, "Good job. Whatever else happened, you got the landlord's attention and helped get the situation taken care of."

MY BROTHERS AND I called my mother's mom Mama. We spent a lot of time at her house, especially after school when my parents were out of town. Mama had this huge stand-alone stereo system that was considerably wider than it was tall. It sat in the corner of her living room, which was the room you came into upon entering her house. You don't see many of these huge stereos for sale any longer. On one side of the stereo—it must have been five feet wide and three and a half feet tall— she kept a vast collection of records of all sizes. In the middle section of the stereo was the radio, and on the far right side was the turntable.

During the summer months we would spend two weeks with my grandmother at her home. She lived in a modest two-bedroom home in a North Memphis community called Klondyke, which was where my mother grew up.

After my family moved to Washington full-time in the fall of 1979, we would spend the summers in Memphis, which in retrospect was insane because Memphis summers are extremely hot and humid. I looked forward to spending time with Mama. Although her house was smaller than ours in Memphis and Washington, there was something very comforting, simple, and warm about her home. She cooked for us, cleaned up after us, and allowed us to do almost anything we wanted in her six-room house and front and backyards. It was at her home that one of the most important lessons a child can learn—the difference between right and wrong—was continually reinforced.

My grandmother had three rules in her house. We weren't allowed to play in the street because a car might hit us; we weren't allowed to walk to the corner store at Claybrook and Vollintine alone because something bad might happen to us without adult supervision; and we weren't allowed to play with certain kids in the neighborhood—namely the boys who were "mannish" and the "fast" girls.

In my grandmother's dictionary, "mannish" meant bad, and "fast" meant sexually precocious. My grandmother would always call my brothers and me mannish when we violated the rules in her house. Mama believed that if you hung around with a bad crowd, you'd become bad. We weren't allowed to spend time with those kids in her neighborhood.

We were still able to play and have fun even with these rules and regulations. And we did. We'd run and race through the house, out through the kitchen, past the refrigerator and freezer where my grandmother kept her meats and the fish we'd catch on summer mornings, out the back door, and down the stairs and back up the driveway to the front porch. We'd start the race over by running through the front door. This was fun at six, seven, eight, and nine. My grandmother taught us how to make homemade ice cream and to fry fish we had just caught, and she introduced us to novel and delicious afternoon delicacies we would eat on the porch. The best one was collard greens, corn bread, and buttermilk all mixed up and served in a bowl like cereal. It was unorthodox but good.

My grandmother had plastic on her sofas and end tables in the living room. It was always clear to my brothers and me when there was trouble in my grandmother's house because all the lights in the house would suddenly turn off. That meant real trouble. It didn't happen often, but it happened often enough.

My grandmother loved her music. One of my chores each morning was to locate and stack my grandmother's favorite 45s on the record player for each to play. She loved James Brown, Johnnie Taylor, Isaac Hayes, Otis Redding, and Al Green. I'd find three or four of the records at a time, place the yellow holder in the middle of the 45 so the record would fit and play on the turntable, and then stack them so that the record player hook would hold each one until the previous record finished. When one record finished and the needle moved out of the way, the next record would drop neatly on top of the other and the needle would return and play it. I would change the records every fifteen or twenty minutes. Trouble would occur if I forgot to change the records, but things only got really bad if we were running and playing so hard in the house that the banging on the floor furnace that separated the living and dining rooms caused one of the 45s to drop on top of a record already playing—which would cause the playing needle to skip and the record to scratch. My sweet little ice-cream-making grandmother didn't like this. Shortly after the record would skip—which really meant we were playing so hard that we "could break something, including an arm or a leg," as Mama would say—the lights in the living room and the stereo would turn off because my grandmother situated the lamps and the stereo in the living room far enough away from electrical out-lets that extension cords were needed to ensure that the lamps got power. And when the music stopped and the lights went out, that usually meant that the extension cords that Mama had bought from the corner drugstore and had neatly wrapped around the wall of the room to power her lamps were being used for a dramatically different purpose from what they were intended. My grandmother didn't hit us too hard with the cords, but she hit us hard enough to remind us of the rules of the house.

I loved and appreciated Mama because, among other things, she helped teach me that rules were important and that actions had consequences. If you followed certain rules, you'd get certain outcomes. Not running with the wrong crowd, not doing drugs and drinking, and doing our homework would likely result in more positive outcomes than the alternative. My grandmother wasn't perfect—and neither was the world she grew up in—but she helped to teach us that life was about making choices. Her hope was that we made more right ones than wrong ones. More than any other reason, her rules were why I never did drugs in high school, college, or law school. To this day, I have never used an illegal drug.

WITH EACH CAMPAIGN, my dad gave me a little more respon-sibility. To my father, though, there was no hierarchy of im-portance when it came to campaign tasks. Putting bumper stickers on cars was just as important as going out and speaking on his behalf. I never stopped doing any of the tasks I had done along the way because my dad never stopped doing them. I remember working on a phone bank during the 1978 campaign. My father was incredibly insistent on thoroughness. He would sit down himself and explain to volunteers exactly how the calling should be done—how to talk to people, what to ask, how many calls to make at a stretch, which staffer to report your results to, and so forth. He wanted his volunteers and staff to understand that phone banking was critically important—and it was. (When I first tried making campaign calls, I didn't realize that there was a problem with saying, "Hi, I'm Harold Ford, Jr. I'm calling from the Harold Ford for Congress campaign. Will you be voting for Harold Ford for Congress?" My dad took me aside and explained the concept of bias. "People won't tell you no once they know you're my son," he explained.)

In 1986, when I was sixteen, I was promoted to junior campaign manager. The title came with no authority. Being a hard worker was a prerequisite, but the promotion's proximate cause seemed to be my new driver's license, which allowed me to take groups out to canvass neighborhoods. I began to help coordinate volunteers and manage the workflow in the office, but like everyone else, I was expected to continue practicing the fundamentals: stickers, signs, door knocks, and calls.

The real difference was that for the first time I was included in the campaign strategy meetings. The conversations would often carry over to our house. I remember sitting in the living room listening to conversations about potential vulnerabilities and the relative merits of different strategies.

Being asked to participate in these discussions was exciting and validating—it signaled a new level of trust in my judgment. Campaign strategy for my dad wasn't about image consultants or opposition researchers or rapid-response ads. The meetings just demonstrated to me more forcefully than ever that his campaigns were extensions of his politics, and the essence of his politics was driven by connection to people and service. My dad was a sophisticated policy thinker and a clever, relentless campaigner who never lost a congressional race, but his notions of connection and service guided every strategic decision he made.

IF THERE WAS a graduation point in my political education, it was not when I reached the level of campaign manager—which was important—but when I was asked to speak in churches on his behalf. The black church had always been my father's base. His relationships with pastors and church leaders were the most important in his life personally and politically. He instituted an office policy as soon as he was elected in 1974: Pastors get immediate access. When pastors called, they were put right through to him. If my father wasn't in the office, his staff had to track him down. In Washington, that sometimes meant finding him on the House floor or getting messages to him while he was in committee hearings. He would excuse himself to take or return the call. He would get upset when his staff didn't find him immediately.

My dad was the only politician I knew who could walk into any church in Memphis and be invited to speak. Pastors acknowledged the attendance of most politicians who came to worship, but when my dad walked in, there was never a question as to whether he was going to be asked to sit in the front pew and be invited to speak. Most politicians invited to give political remarks at church would not be asked to speak from the pulpit. More often than not, other Memphis politicians would speak from the podium in the sanctuary—an honor in and of itself. My dad was always asked to speak from the pulpit.

My father was received this way because he made a point of attending church services year-round, whether he was campaigning or not. Pastors and that particular church family appreciated and remembered that, so when my dad came during campaign season, he was always introduced and invited to speak from the pulpit. And when my dad was invited to sit in the front of the church before speaking, half the time he would politely decline. My mom, brothers, and I were often with him, and unless a pastor insisted that we move up to the front, we sat in the back of the church.

"When you go into a church," he told me, "you don't need to sit in the front. You don't need to speak. You go to worship, listen to the sermon, and pray with and for the community."

I'll never forget overhearing a pastor say to an assistant pastor after service one day when my dad and I were leaving the pastoral study, "That's why I love Harold Ford. He's not like so many of these politicians. He just comes here to worship. Doesn't even want to sit in the front."

And when my dad did speak, he was to the point.

He never abused the time granted him. He would speak for four or five minutes, devoting three of those to thanking and acknowledging the church. He would thank the pastor, the first lady, the church mother board, deacons, ushers, the long-standing members of the church, and the choir. He would recall projects he had worked on with church members and the times people had come to see him in Washington. He would call out names: At times, it seemed like my dad had relationships with literally everybody in the church. I didn't fully understand how one person could know so many people and have affected them so much. I was learning.

Making these kinds of connections was natural for my father—names and relationships flowed into his speech. Because the stories were real and he had established personal connections with each of the people he mentioned, he created bonds even with those he didn't have a relationship with.

He would remind people that Election Day was coming up and thank them for the support they had shown him in years past. He knew when he needed to address specific issues, but he never allowed that to marginalize the living connection, and he was a master at relating issues to people and at laying out how a particular policy was affecting the people to whom he was speaking. I would watch him and watch the congregation. It was amazing. He knew his audience, and even though he was the only one talking—aside from the many "Amen"s heard from the congregation throughout his speech—he was having a conversation with the congregation. As I got older, I thought, "If I get into politics, I want to connect with people like that."

My father used to tell me all the time, "Learn to hold a room. If you hold a room's attention, you can win the room's support."

It's impossible to do what my dad did without a prodigious memory. He always remembered where and how he met people. Fortunately for me, my mother was blessed with the powers of recall as well.

I've been accused of inheriting my dad's political seat. I wished he could have given me the seat. But what I did inherit was my dad's work ethic and memory—which was more important.

The first time my dad sent me out to speak at a Sunday church service was the summer of 1988. I remember it like it was yesterday. I was at Greater Mt. Moriah Baptist Church, in Memphis. I was eighteen years old. I didn't have the relationships my father had with congregations in the district, but I knew the Greater Mt. Moriah congregants and their pastor, J. L. Payne, because my brothers and I had gone to vacation Bible school there.

I got up and thanked everyone, the way my father did, and then I talked about what it had been like attending Bible school at Mt. Moriah and how meaningful it was to come back. I described how tough Pastor Payne had been on us in Bible class. "Who would have thought that a few years later I would be standing at his pulpit?" I said as I looked around wide-eyed with excitement and trepidation. Everybody laughed, and I said, "You taught me well, as you have so many other young people like me, Pastor Payne, and I will always be grateful to you for it." I went on to talk about some of the lessons from vacation Bible study. I reminded Pastor Payne of something he said to the small class one summer morning when I was ten. "Remember, kids, there will always be more Davids than Goliaths. Meaning the Lord always has and always will find an answer for you."

Toward the end of my short speech, people were "Amen"-ing and agreeing with me aloud. It felt good. I didn't have the same effect as my dad, because I didn't know or understand the people in the church as well as my dad did. But I was learning.

ARGUMENTS *of* MY OWN

THE MOVE TO D.C. WHEN I WAS NINE WAS A BIG adjustment for my brothers and me. New school, new neighborhood, new friends, and no cousins or big Sunday dinners. We quickly adjusted, though. We made friends, picked up soccer, and played football, stickball, and basketball with the kids in the neighborhood. The Ford boys all started at Lafayette Elementary, a public school in upper northwest D.C. I graduated from sixth grade in 1982 and headed to St. Albans with a great push from an old family friend and mentor, then senator Al Gore, Jr., himself a graduate of St. Albans.

The six years I spent at St. Albans, from seventh through twelfth grades, awakened me to the power of listening and thinking. By the time I left, I was beginning to form at least precursory opinions about many of the major social issues dominating the political conversation. The older I got, the more I was able to use my nascent political skills, until then confined to my father's campaigns, to bring about a modest expansion of the school's curriculum.

◆　　◆

WHEN I FIRST arrived at St. Albans, in seventh grade, the intensity of the academic demands shocked me. Seventh grade was the most rigorous academic experience during my formative years. I had attended a good public school, but it hadn't come close to preparing me for the rigors of seventh grade at St. Albans. In retrospect, it was like going from elementary school to high school. I didn't appreciate it then, but as I look back on it, our classes were structured like college courses. College and law school were hard in their own ways, sometimes tremendously so, but in relative terms, nothing was more of a shock than my seventh-grade year at St. Albans. Homework took at least three hours a night, six days a week. The volume and complexity of the work were staggering. The reading load was massive. School ended at 2:30, and sports practice began at 2:45. I was finished with practice at 4:30 or 5:00 and was home by 6:00, and I started my homework right after dinner.

The sixty guys in my class were all driven and smart, and many were more prepared than I was. My English teacher, Ron Wilmore, helped me adjust to the new realities. He was the only black teacher I had that first year, and I was one of only a handful of black kids in the seventh grade. It was also my first time in an all-boys academic environment.

Mr. Wilmore was also my toughest teacher. One day he pulled me aside and said, "This will be the roughest academic experience you've ever had, this class of mine. The preparation you're going to have to do for class will be unlike anything you've done before. I don't mean to scare you, but I do mean to scare you—you need to realize what you've taken on. And what I expect from you."

That was important for me to hear. It wasn't a warning—it was an outlining of expectations.

ST. ALBANS FORCED me to see the world through new lenses, and one of the most positive experiences I had was attending Episcopalian services in the school chapel twice a week. My St. Albans worship experiences were far different from the black Baptist services I was used to. Chapel services at St. Albans were more restrained compared to my normal Sunday Baptist services in D.C. and Memphis. The entire congregation—students, professors, and administrators—sang the hymns. Choirs sang them at my Baptist church, and we in the congregation could sing along if we knew the words and wanted to. There was little if any call-and-response at St. Albans, and the services were shorter. To me, this wasn't good or bad. It was just different, and it deepened the development of my faith identity. I came to better understand the importance of prayer. I came to understand more and more that the walls that divide Christians when we pray are man-made. In the words of my personal prayer book, *Sacred Space*, which captures it well, "The secret history of the church is not in the councils, doctrines, crusades, or bishops, still less in churches or cathedrals, but in the body of Christians who pray to the Father through

Jesus Christ His Son: what you might call the contemplative tradition. . . ." St. Albans helped me understand how true this was.

I respected and revered the history of my Baptist faith and the fullness of its turbulence and triumphs, and I still do. But at St. Albans, I gained an appreciation for the spectrum of Christian traditions. Although many students and professors at St. Albans belonged to other religions or Christian denominations, I don't remember any religious tension or anyone feeling uncomfortable about attending chapel services. Yet it was an unambiguously Christian experience.

POLITICS WAS ALWAYS a presence at St. Albans. Many of my classmates' parents were fixtures in Washington's political establishment. My beliefs to that point had been largely shaped by the views of my parents and their friends, which was fine and normal. I absorbed their analysis of the nation's political circumstances fairly passively. When I started at St. Albans in 1982, Ronald Reagan had been president for two years, and I was steeped in anti-Reagan rhetoric from my dad and national Democrats. His policy priorities, namely his willingness to cut social service programs drastically while increasing defense spending by orders of magnitude, were roundly disparaged in my house. I repeated much of the rhetoric I was hearing without fully understanding it. I saw the actions of the Reagan administration, and the workings of government in general, through a very distinct lens—a Democratic one.

But St. Albans forced us to use an array of lenses to make

sense of the world. My classes and classmates challenged me to back up my positions with facts. I started to realize that most of my classmates were products of their upbringing too. Some students clung to rigid political perspectives, but St. Albans urged us to be critical and independent thinkers.

In seventh-grade English class, Mr. Wilmore forced us to explain and defend our interpretations of Orwell's *1984*. A fraction of our overall grade was based on debates and oral presentations, and I did well in that format. In eighth grade, my social studies teacher, Hugh Taft Morales, organized weekly debates on controversial social and political issues. He always assigned us our positions to argue. He would often force us to argue against what was comfortable for us. He forced us to think, and his approach taught and reinforced a strategic lesson: Know your opponent's arguments before entering a debate.

During some of the debates in his class, my personal opinions changed entirely. I will never forget the assignment on debating capital punishment. The question was "Is capital punishment an effective deterrent to violent crime?" I was assigned to argue that it was. Initially, I was uncomfortable. There was ambivalence in my household. My mom was against the death penalty, but my dad never expressed an opinion, which suggested to me that he was open to it. I was opposed because at twelve years old, I had been led to believe that capital punishment was economically and racially discriminatory. The data suggested that poor people and African Americans were more likely to get the death penalty. I wasn't analyzing crime and sociological data in eighth grade, but what I thought

I knew caused me to oppose capital punishment. But I had to argue the opposite.

I was worried about how genuine I would be in making the argument. As I prepared for the debate, two things stood out: first, the right of victims' families to emotional and psychological closure, and second, our society's right to define in absolute terms acceptable moral conduct. I also began to think that safeguards against discriminatory prosecution and inadequate legal representation could be put into place. In the end, deterrence was important but ultimately not decisive for me. It was closure for victims' families.

I lost the capital punishment argument that day, but the assignment caused me to reexamine a variety of my beliefs.

It wasn't until law school that I became a supporter of capital punishment for certain crimes. It was after the bombings at the federal building in Oklahoma City. Timothy McVeigh deserved the death penalty.

We weren't policy wonks in seventh and eighth grades. We were regular kids. We liked sports and we liked girls. But the faculty was careful to plant the seeds, and the older I got, the more interested I became in political discourse and policy. During my junior and senior years at St. Albans, I was admitted to the debate society and the Government Club, and I started engaging more formally in political dialogue.

Membership in the Government Club was limited to the best debaters in a school full of debaters. The club had a liberal team and a conservative team, and to be admitted, a candidate had to be interviewed by members of whichever ideological team he chose. For thirty minutes, a candidate had to field a barrage of pointed policy questions. Club members tested the breadth of a candidate's knowledge, the openness and quickness of one's mind, and the persuasiveness of his presentation. And they wanted to know how hard a potential member was willing to prepare to understand the issues he would be debating. I was reminded how serious the debate club was and how challenging it would be. Some might have called us nerds, but the coolest kids in school wanted to be members. I was admitted my junior year.

The Government Club met every Thursday evening. Students were expected to spend the prior week studying the issue. We argued trade and tax and education policy, the Bork Supreme Court nomination, nuclear proliferation, and sanctions on South Africa. We argued the issues of the day, including abortion, affirmative action, and school prayer. Few issues escaped us. The forty debaters were split into liberal and conservative camps. Before speaking, we had to raise our hands and be recognized by the moderator, Ted Eagles, the chair of the history department. The debates were civil, informed, and intense. Professor Eagles was the glue.

At the end of the evening, we would vote on each side's performance. Our votes weren't bound by ideological affiliations, and despite the even number of people on each side, we rarely ended up with ties. Liberals weren't always convinced by the liberal position, and vice versa.

I was elected president of the liberals my senior year. I started to realize more and more that my political and policy positions cannot be put easily in an ideological box. Sometimes I had to reframe the policy question to make the liberal argument more palatable to me. On some nights, I found myself unable to argue passionately in defense of our liberal position. I was spending a lot of time thinking deeply about issues, and I began to have serious reservations about ideological rigidity, conservative or liberal.

One of the more illuminating debates we had was on U.S. trade policy and economic competitiveness. Specifically, the question was "Did Japan's car-manufacturing prowess, combined with its purchases of U.S. companies and infrastructure, constitute a sufficient threat to America's economic well-being to warrant trade sanctions and regulations on foreign ownership of U.S. assets?" I studied the issue carefully and listened intently to the debate. The club concluded that in a capitalist system, the best ideas and products must be allowed to flourish and prevail. America's answer to stiff economic competition should be to out-innovate our competitors, the winning argument went that night. But there was a compelling argument in favor of tariffs or sanctions to protect our domestic car industry. The U.S. market should be open only to trading partners with comparable industry practices and reciprocal market openness. That argument lost that night.

The debate forced me to think in a different way about America's future as an economic and military superpower. Japan, China, and other emerging nations would inevitably rival us economically and possibly militarily. How could America remain the chief defender of freedom in the world as well as its innovation capital and economic engine? What would we as a nation have to do to remain a superpower?

The quality of America's education system was the key to it all, I concluded. Ultimately the nation's competitiveness was tied to improving education outcomes. Crime rates, I believed, were largely linked to poor education options. I had accepted without challenge the notion that alternative education financing structures, like vouchers, ran counter to sound education policy. I readily accepted the argument that vouchers and other education reform programs directed scarce public money away from schools serving some of the nation's academically neediest kids to an amorphous capitalistic education network more motivated by potential profits for investors in private education companies than by student achievement. I routinely argued against education reform. A particularly heated debate on the issue of education reform occurred one Thursday evening in Government Club. And then a question was asked by my classmate that changed my thinking on education reform.

"If you were a parent without much money," a fellow student said, "and your kid was forced to go to a bad public school, what options would you have? This is what education reform must fix."

New strategies and approaches would be needed to address this problem. My basic political orthodoxies were being reshaped, but I didn't view my new thinking as a betrayal of the Democratic Party or liberal politics, as I understood them at the time. I viewed it more as a real and growing commitment to outcomes, as opposed to a fidelity to ideology. The achievement gap between blocs of kids in America could largely be defined by the educational choices or options available to them. Too many kids lacked choice and opportunity, and that wasn't fair to them or the rest of us. Without an opportunity to be challenged, corrected, encouraged, and tested mentally and physically in school as I was at St. Albans, the chances for long-term professional and personal success in life were limited for kids, I thought. Of equal concern, if these kids didn't succeed in life, it was likelier that they would become a financial burden on society by draining public resources. Public school choice didn't exist in 1986, and Teach for America wasn't born until 1990. The one size fits all approach in education was failing the nation.

These were my first lessons that politics was about problem solving, not about the imposition of a correct ideology. Doctrines were not indispensable to positive outcomes. In fact, rigidity was a precursor to failure when one was searching for answers to hard policy questions. It seemed to me that no single viewpoint contained all the solutions, and I gradually stopped using traditional liberal-conservative paradigms to define problems and find answers.

What ultimately resonated with me was a question that I ask of myself: How do we make things work better?

DURING MY SENIOR year, I took a required class called omnibus history, a bundling of European and American history. Several of my classmates and I were struck by the near-absence of study of Africa and Asia. We thought the course should be broadened to include studying people of color or that the class title should be changed to reflect the actual reach of the class. Ultimately, we wanted the former.

Simultaneously, there was a movement for multicultural academic expansion happening around the country at the time. Elite colleges and universities were creating multicultural studies departments. People were becoming increasingly aware of the role African Americans had played in American history, and they consequently recognized their underrepresentation in standard coursework.

Along with a brilliant and creative classmate, Ryan Lloyd, I believed that the most effective way to bring about the change we wanted would not be to organize protests, but to draft a proposal to the school curriculum committee to incorporate study of African, Asian, and African American history and literature into the broader curriculum. Once we decided to work within the confines of the institution, we needed to understand its protocols. As we worked on the proposal, which took us several weeks, we studied the makeup of the faculty committee and the curriculum-reform process. We had to convince a particular group of people to do a particular thing in a particular way. We asked ourselves, What would the administration be receptive to? What would the students be receptive to? Who, in other words, were our constituencies? What would our opposition say? We needed to anticipate their answers and have better ones. Dr. Taft Morales would be proud of my approach.

Ryan and I had met in seventh grade. I practically grew up in his house in Potomac; his mom was a second mom to me, and his brother and sister were like mine. Ryan enjoyed the same treatment and care in my home from my mom and family. We were best friends. We wanted as many students as possible to benefit from the changes. So who would resist that, we thought.

The obvious solution—hiring a new professor with experience teaching African American history and literature and creating a new series of courses—posed real problems. Aside from the expense and requisite reorganization, there were only 300 kids in the upper school (ninth to twelfth grades), so there would probably be a relatively small number of interested students. Given that and the demands of the curriculum, the additional classes would have to be mandatory if many people were going to take them. We knew that a new mandatory class wouldn't win a lot of faculty support—or student support.

And we weren't big alumni donors with hundreds of thousands of dollars to give to the school in exchange for a new academic chair or course of study. Interestingly, that happened as we were strategizing and working on our multicultural project. Several alums raised a lot of money for the creation of an Asian Studies Chair at St. Albans. It was immediately embraced.

Ryan and I were envious of that kind of support, but we knew that money for our project wasn't forthcoming. We decided to meet individually with the headmaster, a week ahead of the curriculum committee vote, thinking that if we approached him calmly and rationally we would get an agreement right at the outset that our cause at least merited serious consideration. It would have been a lot easier to forgo these meetings with the faculty and walk into the curriculum committee meeting brandishing a check for a million dollars for a multicultural studies chair. Again, that wasn't going to happen.

Most of the curriculum committee members were not shy about expressing their concerns. Some faked interest; others were less ambiguous. One or two had no interest at all in the idea. The chair of the math department clearly believed there were more pressing priorities. I was in his advanced math class at the time. There were fewer than ten students in that class, so I took advantage of his accessibility to gain insight into what could persuade him. I'd catch him before or after class. He was pretty blunt.

He had little patience for a separate class. He would listen to my arguments and consistently say flatly, "Yes, I don't know how we can add another class." Without meaning to further our cause, he helped me understand that when you add a class to the curriculum, you also add a lot of work for the faculty. He thought a new permanent class would strain faculty resources, and that view was shared broadly by his colleagues. And he voiced some other reservations. I knew that we wouldn't be able to sell everyone, but he revealed the arguments he was going to make to the other members of the committee. He was influential—that I knew.

After more conversations with him, Ryan and I concluded that we should propose incorporating our ideas into existing classes. It would improve our chances of winning approval if we took the separate class idea off the table.

We presented our case before the committee in the headmaster's office. It was the two of us standing before the ten people on the committee. They were assembled around a conference table. I knew they thought we would be intimidated. All of the school's department heads were there, the same people responsible for grading us at the end of the semester. But I wasn't afraid or intimidated. It helped that Skip Grant was present. Coach Grant was the conscience of St. Albans—he still is today. He also was the only African American member of the committee.

The argument was simple. Ryan had written it and I was to deliver it.

The reality is, we're not learning American history thoroughly. We aren't exploring the very meaningful role blacks have played in the development of the American political system or American culture. Among the touchstones of omnibus history are the Great Depression and the Civil War, and in both cases we look at African Americans in passive roles as victims. While we can't ignore that, we can't allow it to be the sum total of the African American experience as presented in the course. We're missing a broader story here. There's a component of blacks' involvement in the country that's much bigger, more meaningful, and more positive. Why wouldn't we explore, if only briefly, the nature of the West African societies from which American slaves came? Why not look at how those cultures eventually informed and transformed American culture? Why not study the role of jazz in the evolution of authentic American music? Why not read Wright and Baldwin in eleventh-grade English and then study the Harlem Renaissance as we discuss the civil rights movement? And this can all be done in our existing curriculum. And it would make the entire student body more informed.

It went well. The most important validation for me was what Coach Grant said to us in private after the presentation.

You-all really surprised the committee. You didn't come in and give an emotional or theatrical presentation. You came in with a smart and measured approach: "Here's what we consider to be the problem, and here's how we're suggesting you solve it without disrupting the curriculum or class schedule or increasing the faculty's workload." The committee was really impressed that you had antici-pated those issues, and addressed their concerns before they even voiced them. I was proud of you, and I know your parents would be as well.

Regardless of the outcome, Coach Grant's validation was most important to me. In the end, the curriculum was broad-ened and everyone benefited—and still do. I was learning.

The FACE *of* ONE'S CAUSE

O N MY FIRST DAY AT THE UNIVERSITY OF PENN-
sylvania, my father did something I'll never forget. I
had been assigned to a dorm called Hill House, and
my parents and brothers were helping me move in. My mom
and I were getting my things situated and cleaning the room
while my dad was out running some errands on campus. My
mother was organizer in chief. She was determined to make
the tiny dorm room a decent place for her oldest son to study
and live in. My mom knew I wouldn't cook in the common
area on my dorm floor, so she was relieved that one of the campus's largest dining halls was on the first floor of the dorm
building. That worked for me, too.

Suddenly, my father reappeared. He was carrying a very
large University of Pennsylvania flag, and without saying anything, he proceeded to hang it on the wall. My dorm room was
small, and the flag dominated the space on my side of the
room, which I shared. Beneath the "University of Pennsylvania" lettering was the number "1992"—my graduation year.

I was slightly perturbed. I had wanted to put up posters. It was a nice-looking flag, but I probably wouldn't have chosen it or hung it where he did. It was the kind of thing I might have sent home to my parents to hang in the family room or on a pole on the front porch before a Penn-Princeton basketball game.

My dad said, "What do you think?"

I said, "Look, it's . . . I like it."

He said, "Good. I want you to see that flag every morning when you wake up." There was no way I could miss seeing it.

He didn't say it harshly. I just thought perhaps he had been infected with the school spirit—a lot of it. The campus was full of excited parents and freshmen; the atmosphere of hope and possibility was contagious. I didn't want to say anything to dampen his or my mother's spirits. Plus, they were paying my tuition, and I was grateful.

My father said, "I want you to see '1992' every morning when you wake up, because after that, I'm not paying one dime for you to go to college. You need to understand that." Again, there was no harshness in his voice, and he couldn't conceal his pride. I said, "Yes, sir. I'll see it every morning—even if I don't want to."

I got the message. He had been looking forward to this moment for a long time, and it was meaningful to him. When he and his eleven brothers and sisters had successfully put themselves through college, it had been a tremendous family achievement. My dad worked his way through college waiting tables, parking cars, and driving home from Nashville to Memphis on the weekends to manage funerals at the family funeral home. N.J. and Vera, with their great belief in the transformative power of education but without the resources to fully pay for their children's tuition, had been exceptionally proud. I was acutely aware of this history, and I was taking nothing for granted. Like many kids, I worked for weekend money. I started out as a student security guard in campus dormitories and then became a student security supervisor. And like my dad, I valeted cars and waited tables. The difference was, I only did it for extra spending money.

ONE OF THE biggest issues confronting the university when I arrived on campus was cultural diversity training. Penn had declined to make the training mandatory for freshmen. As I was getting acclimated to college life, the issue was percolating all around me. There were protests across campus in favor of compulsory diversity training. I agreed that diversity training should be obligatory, and I wanted to help. It reminded me of Ryan's and my work at St. Albans. One way to participate, I thought, would be to serve on the Penn Student Senate. As an elected member, I could influence the conversation, I believed.

Soon after I got to Penn, I started campaigning to be one of the freshman representatives on the senate. I saw right away that I could employ very basic campaign tactics and be effective. The race would be more determined by outreach to students than by substance. Newly arrived eighteen-year-old freshmen are focused on making friends and getting into important and popular classes and enjoying the freedoms of unparented life, more so than on talking campus politics right away. They're generally not preoccupied with campus policymaking. So there was no need to have a well-defined policy identity. The students who voted chiefly wanted to make sure that the candidates weren't idiots. The only issues I was passionate about were the need for diversity training, extending the drop-add period, and adding spots to some of the more popular freshman classes. That was the platform. I had opponents, and I had to assess their strengths and weaknesses and figure out where my support was going to come from. There are constants to any campaign.

First of all, I needed to connect with as many people as I could. I had watched the way other people were campaigning. They were too serious. They were dressed up and standing outside dorms handing out pamphlets. They were walking around campus making speeches. That's what students expect politicians to do. Most people did not want to be randomly accosted by student candidates full of nervous and awkward campus political talk.

I campaigned in casual clothes, went wherever people were hanging out, and explained my reasons for running conversationally. In such a gentle campaign landscape, meeting people in a natural manner and establishing a personal connection with them would be by far the best way to work. Conversely, it seemed comical to put on a suit and fleetingly transmit information to passing students. And given how I had learned to campaign, that seemed unnatural. Even at eighteen, I believed that if I could meet you and talk to you, I could convince you to vote for me.

The one thing everybody was spending a lot of time on

was socializing, so the more I integrated my campaign into the social life of the campus, the more access I would have to people.

Then there was the ground game. The majority of our class lived in one of two places: the Quad or Hill House. The majority of the freshman class lived in the Quad.

I was campaigning with a good friend, Daryl Anderson, who was also a candidate, and we initially focused, as everyone did, on our own dorm. We were lucky that Hill House was near several important academic buildings, including the athletic complex and the engineering school, so its dining hall drew people from many parts of campus. I calculated that, given the expected turnout rate and the size of our class (about 2,200), I could finish in the top twelve just by persuading enough people in the Hill House dining hall to vote for me.

The candidates from the Quad had almost no presence in Hill House. They tended to spend their time, when they weren't out campaigning on campus, shoring up support on their own floors and in their own dorms, thinking that would be enough. For some, it was, but during my first month in school, I had formed relationships with people across campus. That proved to be valuable.

I enlisted the help of everyone I knew, including one of my best friends from high school, who was extremely outgoing and lived in the Quad. My friends introduced me to their friends, and often, after talking to me, the more gregarious of them would volunteer to ask people to vote for me. Socializing came naturally to me—it wasn't difficult or embarrassing for me to start a conversation with a group of total strangers. I kept moving out toward the edges of fresh social circles, and my campaign ended up with a little more reach than the other campaigns.

There was another reason it made sense to leverage social networks. When people run for political office, they and their constituents live in a similar community, and many for a long time. But the students at Penn had never lived in the community before. We had all just arrived, and we were still trying to figure out how the place worked. Anyone voting would likely rely on what they heard from friends in their dorm. If someone on their hall, whom they liked and were spending a lot of time with, said, "Hey, have you been following this thing? I heard about this guy Harold Ford—we should go vote for him," they probably would.

I was thinking that given the nature of relationships in this environment, those were the kinds of conversations I had to initiate, directly or indirectly. I needed people to be saying to their friends, "Hey, I know this guy. He seems like a good guy." It wouldn't take much more than that.

As the vote approached, I began trying to turn one vote into two, or more. If I could get 200 or 300 votes, I was going to make the top twelve. I asked people to tell their friends to vote. Given the number of votes in play, if they could get three or four of their friends to vote, it would make a big difference. I would say, "Get three people who don't know me to vote for me. When you're walking to the polling place, grab two of your friends from class and take them over."

Unfortunately, I had to be out of town on the day of the

election for a family event, but I called Daryl every thirty minutes that evening trying to get the results.

"They haven't released any numbers yet—we don't know," Daryl said the first time I called him. "We still don't have any numbers," he told me thirty minutes later. "We're going to get them soon," he said a few calls after that. Finally, I called back and he said, "You're not going to believe this." I thought, "Man, that means we didn't make it. Maybe we came in fifteenth or sixteenth as opposed to tenth or eleventh or twelfth."

"It's good news. It's interesting news," Daryl said.

"What's the good news?" I asked.

"We're both in."

"What's the interesting news?"

"You finished first."

I was pleasantly surprised. The first-place finisher got to serve on the faculty senate as the sole freshman representative. My strategy had paid off.

I LEARNED SOME valuable lessons right away on the faculty senate. Most of the faculty believed themselves to be very important and wanted to be listened to—so I listened and listened. I didn't talk at all for the first few meetings. I wanted to understand the issues, personalities, and politics of the senate. I realized very early that Penn's president, Sheldon Hackney, who presided over the body, was the most powerful force in the room, but he didn't have all the power. There were, like there are in every political body, other circles of power. It would be important to develop relationships in those circles as well.

People began making presentations about the importance of the freshman diversity seminar. On campus, the issue continued to heat up. The local Philadelphia news media started covering it; student groups were marching and protesting. If the seminar wasn't mandatory, supporters argued, students would avoid it. Given the time demands placed on them, freshmen were not going to be inclined to attend the classes unless they were compulsory. Students would have skipped most of freshman orientation if they hadn't been required to attend, many believed. So the administration could signal its seriousness only by making the classes mandatory.

One of the things that continually surprised me was how many of my white classmates had never really interacted with black people day to day before arriving at Penn, and vice versa. We had all learned to self-segregate. When you see kids who don't look like you and who talk and act and dress a little differently, there's reason to be reluctant to socialize without some organizing force helping. Students had retreated to safe, homogenous havens. Many black students spent most of their time with black students, and most of the white students did the same. I socialized and talked with everyone. I had grown up in a more racially diverse setting and was entirely comfortable in this environment. In fact, it was the intensity of this new dynamic that was strange to me.

I was involved with many of the student groups pressing for a university-led diversity seminar for freshmen because I believed the more time we spent together, the more we'd realize how much we had in common. I would listen to both sides and try to persuade intransigents. One problem was that some supporters on campus had become very emotional about the issue. I think there's room for people to make a big noise about issues, but it can be counterproductive. I would always ask myself, What is the most effective way to bring the people closest to our position all the way to us?

In the faculty senate, I was finding that many of the faculty favored the compulsory diversity seminar. The faculty were deeply concerned about divisions on campus and wanted to unite the campus by doing the right thing. Most of the faculty were uncomfortable with the polarizing tone of the debate. Many of the professors on the senate had been activists themselves in college and understood the value of activism. But they also understood activism's limits. They wanted inclusiveness; they wanted any new initiative to be as collaborative an effort as possible. And they wanted a consensus. We could make a strong appeal to them, but we had to broaden the coalition and moderate the tone of the debate.

Some of my classmates grew louder and louder, and I argued that more aggressive tactics only worked to a point. We were gaining support with the faculty senate. But faculty senate members didn't want to look like they were giving in to the demands of radical student groups. They didn't want to be seen as caving in to groups whose members they perceived as loudmouths. The faculty worried that the campus newspaper would portray them as having been bulldozed by black activists on campus.

Thankfully, there were two influential and mature upperclassmen whom all the activist groups respected, Tracy Miller and Seth Berger. Seth was a graduate of a prestigious New York City private school. Tracy was a smart and polished Baltimore public school product whose understanding of politics exceeded just about everyone's on campus. Her education in national politics had been sharpened the previous year by her involvement in Jesse Jackson's presidential campaign. Their leadership and partnership were more important than anything else. I followed their lead. Ultimately, the senate agreed, and diversity won—that evening.

Tracy and Seth were a great team. They understood the strength of their union around this issue. She said, "It'll be surprising and persuasive to have a Jewish kid who went to Horace Mann making the coalition's demands, as opposed to a black kid from Brooklyn." And she knew that she and Seth together would create a picture of diversity and inclusiveness. She reinforced that by reaching out to and gaining the participation of Hispanic and Asian American student groups. She understood that sometimes, you let someone else be the face of your cause in order to win. She and Seth put together exactly the kind of coalition that the faculty members on the senate wanted to see—and needed to see.

JESSE JACKSON'S CAMPAIGN had transformed American politics by reintroducing the power of grassroots activism. Reverend Jackson's Rainbow Coalition gave a voice to millions of people from all racial, ethnic, and economic backgrounds. His rise as a national political figure inspired a generation of young leaders, including me, to have the courage to ask for what was fair and right. In high school, my exposure to Reverend Jackson was personal and direct because his youngest son, Yusef, who remains my closest friend today, was my classmate. During my senior year, I had the opportunity to travel with Yusef to his father's campaign events in Washington, D.C., Philadelphia, Chicago, and New York. Reverend Jackson's presidential campaigns—the first one was in 1984—cleared a path for many aspiring young politicians to pursue office at every level. The massive voter registration drives Reverend Jackson engineered across the South between his '84 and '88 presidential campaigns paved the path to victory for many Senate Democrats in 1986 and allowed Senate Democrats to reclaim the majority. It was Reverend Jackson's work between '84 and '88 that propelled his candidacy in '88 and sparked activism on college campuses across the country—he even paved the way for David Dinkins to be elected the first black mayor in New York City and Doug Wilder to be elected governor of Virginia in 1989. This was a big part of what inspired Ryan and me at St. Albans.

DURING THE SECOND half of my freshman year at Penn, tensions between black students on campus and Penn's daily newspaper worsened. Whether it was intentional or not, Penn's newspaper, the *Daily Pennsylvanian*, didn't fairly cover black student events on campus.

. Although diversity training was mandatory it would not start until the following school year. It couldn't come soon enough. When the paper covered black activities on campus, it routinely misspelled names, got basic facts wrong, and distorted the spirit and even the purpose of meetings and events. Student reporters would come to meetings of African American organizations for brief stays and write incomplete stories. Oftentimes, the content and substance of meetings were mischaracterized.

Because the student reporters would only stay a few minutes, their articles missed the real purpose of meetings. The paper used negative language to describe the mood of black student organizations, which created the worst impressions on campus. The coverage didn't foster better relations between student groups.

My answer to the problem was for us in the Black Student League (BSL) to be more press-savvy. I told them that when reporters came to meetings, we should have a press release outlining the main purpose of the meeting, and then give the press the name of one person to call for follow-up. I reminded my classmates that sometimes our BSL meetings ran long and reporters have to leave to file stories before deadline. In short, we needed a concise message that would be hard for the newspaper to distort or take out of context.

The second suggestion was that some of us should write for the daily newspaper. I believed someone needed to lead by example, so I applied to be a biweekly columnist for the *Daily Pennsylvanian*. My main faculty adviser was Dr. Harold Haskins. He advised many students. I asked him what he thought of my applying to write a column for the daily newspaper. Dr. Haskins, who looked like a much taller black Einstein, responded, "That's brilliant." That was his favorite response. He had a way of always making you feel good about your decisions.

My thinking was simple—what better way for the *Daily Pennsylvanian* to understand black students than to have more black students write or provide opinions for the newspaper? In my application essay, I shared with the student editors that my political perspective had been shaped by a variety of things: growing up in politics in Memphis and Washington, attending both public and private schools, going to church on Sunday, and believing that finding answers was more important than fighting. Thankfully, I was selected as a columnist for the first semester of my sophomore year.

I wrote on campus issues. I wrote about national political issues. My perspective sometimes ran counter to mainstream views on campus; and sometimes I was squarely in the mainstream. It was important, I believed, to take everyone to task when they were wrong. I was an equal opportunity offender on campus. I wanted to be consistent. I enjoyed writing the column so much that it served as a catalyst for another writing project—cofounding the monthly black student newspaper on campus with a classmate named Antoine Scarborough.

From the outset, we deliberately didn't ask for university support—we wanted to have the independence to say whatever we wanted. The intent was not to espouse contrarian political views, but to be able to challenge authorities on campus when we believed they were not acting in the best interests of students, especially minority students. Our goal was to provoke broader thinking about some of the challenges facing the entire student body.

I quickly learned that publishing a newspaper required significant resources and that we would have to run it like a small business. We drew up a budget, sought funding from individual donors, and went out and pitched advertisers. Blessedly, two of my father's colleagues in Congress—Bill Clay from Missouri, and Lou Stokes from Ohio—each sent me $500 each to start the paper. My parents sent $500, too. I hadn't set out to learn how to run a business, but I did—albeit a small one.

We started out with no staff and no office, but I recruited my friend Gabrielle Glore to be the managing editor of the *Vision*. An upperclass woman, Gabi gave us credibility with students and faculty. We needed it. We worked out of my apartment, which I shared with three others: Daryl Anderson, Bobby Elliott, and Rafaa McRae. All of us worked on the paper from the beginning. Printing costs were high. I would make the thirty-minute drive to the printer's in my Honda Accord and load the papers in the trunk. Then, the four of us would each take a section of campus and distribute the papers by hand.

In a monthly, you can't do much hard news reporting, so the *Vision* was predominantly a paper of commentary. We interpreted and analyzed the events that had occurred over the previous thirty days. I was a big fan of *Black Enterprise* and *Ebony*, and I thought of the *Vision* as a combination of the two, so the content guidelines were flexible. We had a creative writing section. We had a page of poetry. We encouraged all students to express themselves however they saw fit, which was the primary goal. My classmate and childhood friend—and son of the publisher of *Black Enterprise*—Michael Graves advised us on the start of the paper as well. The *Vision* is still alive and well today.

ONE OF THE more memorable moments of activism on campus was after the Rodney King verdict was announced. It was my junior year. The four Los Angeles police officers tried for brutally beating King were found innocent of all charges by a predominantly white jury in Simi Valley, California. The verdict sparked riots and protests across the country. Penn was no exception.

To protest the verdict, a group of us at Penn marched from campus to City Hall chanting, "No justice, no peace!" We were angry, frustrated, and scared. Nerves were raw. The videotape of the police officers beating King was so graphic that it seemed to foreclose the possibility of acquittal. Regardless of where one stood politically, it was hard to understand the verdict.

Our march was loud and, by Penn standards, large—about 700 people at the start. We remained organized and civil. By the time we reached City Hall and turned around, it was dark. On the way back to campus, we had to pass the house of President Hackney, and a spontaneous desire arose among the marchers to wake him and have him address us. We wanted to see if he agreed with us.

As we approached the president's house, I said to my classmates, "Let me handle this. Let me go knock on the door and bring him out."

President Hackney was a decent guy. His national reputation for a commitment to racial equality and civil rights was well known. He knew me from my work on campus, and when we were out raising startup money for the *Vision*, he and his wife had personally contributed $250. His house had a side door and a front door. I walked up the driveway and knocked on the side door. President Hackney was still up, though in his pajamas and robe, and he let me in.

He asked what was going on, and I told him about the march to City Hall in response to the King verdict. I said that our numbers had diminished somewhat after we left City Hall but there was still a big group outside demanding to speak with him. He could hear the chants outside as we were talking.

The president said, "Look, I believe the decision was an outrage. How the jury could clear those police officers is confusing at best."

"Students are obviously upset about this," I said, "and you obviously understand that. If you're comfortable saying what you just said, I would encourage you to say that. Students will appreciate it." I continued, "When you urge people to remain calm, you ought to say, 'Although the system didn't yield the result we wanted at this level, the Justice Department is already exploring other ways to ensure that justice is served here. And if this university can help, we will.' "

The president and I walked out on the porch. I was standing slightly behind President Hackney and to the side. I said, "Everybody, the president has decided to come out and say a few words. Let's give him our attention." The president was still in his robe but had put on a pair of khakis. He spoke well. We the students were satisfied.

President Hackney and I remained friends. I'll never forget when he came to my graduation party, which my parents held for me at a restaurant on campus. He took my father aside and said, "Your son and I are great friends. He's been good for Penn." My dad responded, "Penn's been good for him."

I WAS FORTUNATE enough to hear Bill Clinton speak for the first time at Penn. It didn't seem like an event of enormous import at the time, but it was. This was early in the presidential primary, and the general public wasn't entirely familiar with him yet. He was low in the polls.

Clinton spoke at the Annenberg School of Communications to a group of about one hundred students and faculty, and he was impressive. His argument was simple: The Democratic party had to stand up for the forgotten middle class. The middle class had been left behind, he argued. Clinton was pro-business and pro-trade. He was committed to a new Democratic philosophy that rested on important pillars: community, responsibility, and opportunity. I liked what I was hearing. My good friend Craig Kirby was traveling with Clinton in Philadelphia. Craig had managed to get me on the stage for Clinton's speech that day.

Clinton was talking a different Democratic language. He reminded me of one of my Tennessee political mentors, Al Gore. But Clinton had more of an edge. He almost sounded like a black preacher when he spoke of his upbringing. He was unlike most Democrats in that he spoke openly about his faith, he was completely comfortable in churches, and he wasn't afraid to discuss the need for greater economic opportunity for blacks and other minority groups. But he spoke about these issues not as an add-on but as a part of his main message. It was my politics.

That day at the Annenberg School of Communications, President Clinton gave voice to a lot of the ideas that I was beginning to formulate. In my lifetime, he was the first Democratic presidential nominee who effectively articulated my economic and social values. He was redefining national Democratic politics for the better.

But it wasn't until Clinton's nomination acceptance speech the following year at the Democratic National Convention that I fully appreciated how transformative his politics would be for my generation. I listened to him and said to myself, "That's the kind of Democrat I am." The icing on the cake was when he selected Gore as his running mate.

I had been to a lot of conventions with my family, but this was the first time I had listened to a nominee speak and walked away saying, "This is the guy. This is the guy who speaks for the party. This is a winning message."

TRIAL *and* ERROR

THE U.S. ATTORNEY FOR THE WESTERN DISTRICT of Tennessee, Hickman Ewing, began investigating my father in 1982. I was twelve. After empaneling a grand jury, Ewing's office immediately began leaking their side to the press. My father, Ewing claimed, had taken bribes from the heads of a Knoxville bank to secure federal funds and favors for the bankers and their projects.

My father stated his innocence publicly and repeatedly. He even did the unusual: He volunteered to appear before the grand jury. He said he had nothing to hide and wanted to clear his name. Each time he asked to go before the grand jury, Ewing refused.

For years, the prosecutor failed to convince a grand jury in Memphis that my father had done anything wrong. They refused to indict for almost five years. There was steady coverage in the Memphis press about the investigation, most of it negative. The source was always the U.S. attorney's office. My dad never talked about this with us kids. I would hear him talk about it with others. It was easier for my brothers and me not to see the press coverage because we were in D.C. But we saw it during the summers in Memphis.

I remember seeing cartoons in the Memphis *Commercial Appeal* about the investigation. Most of the jokes were at my father's expense.

My dad didn't seem bothered by the coverage. In fact it seemed to make him more determined to do his job. He worked longer hours. He attended more events all across the district. He wanted the public to know that he didn't fear the U.S. attorney because he was innocent.

At that time, the Reagan Justice Department was launching investigations into and indicting numerous black elected officials across the country. A striking number of federal grand juries were targeting black politicians. Independent legal groups tracked the cases, and the trend was unmistakable.

My dad firmly believed that the investigation was racially and politically motivated. I agreed with him. The numbers don't lie. At one point, it seemed as if half of the Congressional Black Caucus and a score of black mayors were under federal investigation or indictment. My father's passionate opposition to Reagan's agenda probably didn't help.

State politics probably played an even larger role. The institution in question was called United American Bank, which was owned and run by two brothers, Jake and C. H. Butcher. The Butchers were major figures in the national Democratic Party, having supported virtually every important Democratic politician in the South. They were close to Jimmy Carter, who had nearly appointed Jake Butcher chair of the Democratic

National Committee. Carter had also offered Jake a cabinet position—secretary of commerce—but Butcher had declined. The state's Republican governor didn't like the Butchers—probably because Jake was wealthy, good-looking, and a political threat to him. Jake had run for governor twice.

My father and Jake Butcher met in 1970, when both were serving in the Tennessee legislature. They were young, smart, and ambitious, and they became good friends and political allies. They believed in government's ability to help people, and they cosponsored bills to expand aid for students, low-income families, and veterans. Jake and his family spent time in Memphis with our family, and we spent time at Jake's home in Knoxville.

For Tennessee Republicans, prosecuting the Butchers was more than an opportunity to weaken Democrats—it was a chance to try to kill the Tennessee Democratic Party. Ewing, who would go on to become a Whitewater prosecutor under Ken Starr, put all of his office's resources into the case against the Butchers and my dad.

For sure, United American Bank was in the wrong. Both Butcher brothers were convicted of fraud and went to jail.

The specific allegation against my dad was that he took bribes disguised as bank loans from Jake and C. H. Butcher in exchange for securing federal funds for a bridge connecting downtown Memphis and Mud Island, a commercially valuable piece of land in the Mississippi River. The Butchers owned the island and had planned to develop it for commercial and residential purposes. My dad had no involvement with the project.

It was not until 1986 that the investigation really became a part of my life. My dad had a strong opponent in the Democratic primary who explicitly used the investigation against him. I began to appreciate the impact the allegations were having politically. Up to that point, most of my father's primary opponents had been weak and less serious people, but Walter Evans was a credible, intelligent, Harvard-trained African American lawyer.

Evan's campaign theme was "Ford's time is up." He couldn't come out and say, "Harold Ford is a crook. Vote for me." Instead, he argued that the district deserved a change because voters needed someone they could trust. My dad never talked to me about the role of the investigation in the campaign—but I realized it was something he was having to take seriously. I was helping with the campaign—largely working with the street teams, putting up yard signs and putting bumper stickers on cars—and I remember sitting in our living room in Memphis, listening to my father and his advisers discussing whether my father should debate Walter. My dad wanted to demonstrate his grasp of policy issues in Washington and his encyclopedic understanding of his congressional district, but some of his closest advisers were arguing against the debate. They believed it would give Evans a bigger platform than he would ever get otherwise to broadcast his views. In short, my dad had nothing to gain by agreeing to a televised debate: Even if he won the debate on the merits, he couldn't help but give Evans—a well-educated and well-spoken guy—a real chance to appeal to voters. The televised debate didn't happen. My dad beat him like a drum, using the same approach he did in every previous race. He outworked and outsmarted him.

The grand jury at that point had been sitting for four years. My father and his lawyers were amazed that the prosecution had kept it seated so long. The joke is that you can indict a ham sandwich with a grand jury because the prosecution is granted wide procedural latitude and the target of the grand jury isn't entitled to respond. As the years passed, the prosecution's rationale for the investigation kept changing. The only thing that didn't change was the leaking from the U.S. attorney's office.

For more than four and a half years, Ewing had tried to bring an indictment against my father in Memphis. He failed, so finally, he tried in Knoxville, the hometown of the Butcher bank. Within hours of seating the grand jury in Knoxville, Ewing got his indictment. It was a terrible day.

I'll never forget coming home from school on the spring day that the indictment was announced. My dad was there, and his chief of staff and lawyer were as well. Reporters had gathered outside the house. I walked in, and my parents and brothers and I had our first sit-down meeting about the case. I can't imagine how painful this was for my dad, but he showed a strength and courage and toughness that inspires me to this day.

"I've done nothing wrong," he said to us, "and now I will have to prove it in court. And I will. I never thought a day like this would come, or wanted it to come, but Harold, Jake, and Isaac, understand one thing: You have nothing to be ashamed of. Hold your heads up high today and tomorrow."

As he left the room to face the press, his lawyer asked him, "You sure you don't want me to go out and talk to them on your behalf?"

"You forget I've been in politics for seventeen years," my dad answered. "I've never ducked the press. And I'm not going to start now."

"I understand," his lawyer said. "Let's just go over what you're going to say."

They put their heads together for a few minutes, and then my father stepped outside. We watched from the kitchen window.

"What happened today is unfortunate," he said to the reporters. "These charges couldn't be more baseless. Not a single charge is true. This is about a politically motivated prosecutor willing to disregard the law where it serves the interests of the Republican Party. It's shameful, and I will fight these charges and clear my name."

I sat down with my dad's lawyer. He said, "Your dad is going to win this fight. He's going to prove everything he needs to prove, and he's going to make life better for a lot of people when he beats the Justice Department. So when you go back to school tomorrow, and you see this on the front page of the papers, keep your head up."

My mother was crying, but my dad's demeanor didn't change, which gave me great comfort. It allowed me to think of the indictment as another fight my dad had to win. Politically, he was always in a fight.

My father had to mount a political defense as well as a legal defense. He had to convince his constituents that he had done nothing wrong and that this would not affect his standing in Congress or his ability to deliver services to his constituents. Already, damage had been done: When he was indicted, he lost his subcommittee chairmanship of the Ways and Means Committee. To his supporters, he said, "For the prosecutors, this is all politics. That's all it is. If I were not black and a Democrat, this would not be happening." I believed him.

I took my father's strength for granted then, but the older I got, the more I understood how powerful a blow this was to him and to my parents' relationship. The case created financial and emotional strains we as a family still reel from, and it eventually led to the dissolution of my parents' marriage.

But when I was with my father, I didn't see any change in him. The only change was circumstantial. He began going back to Memphis more frequently, and my mother and brothers and I began spending more time in Washington.

The next morning, news of the indictment made the front page of all the papers. At St. Albans, my classmates asked me about it. They asked out of curiosity. I wanted to tell them that the allegations were false. I was probably a little more verbose than I should have been in responding during that first week or two after the news broke. I was learning more details about the case, overhearing my dad's conversations with his lawyers, and asking questions. At school, I offered thorough, ardent defenses of my dad. One day, Skip Grant and Reverend Will Billow, the school chaplain, pulled me aside and Billow said, "Harold, you don't need to go into this kind of detail. I'm watching you and listening to you, and I know it bothers you, but you don't need to get into it this way. Answer quickly and move on. Your dad didn't do anything wrong. Just say so and move on."

SHORTLY AFTER THE indictment, my dad's lawyers requested that the trial be moved to Memphis from Knoxville. The judge agreed. A steady stream of motions and countermotions and delays pushed the trial date back by several years. Sometimes my father and his lawyers had to wait for weeks or months for court responses. I got updates from time to time at college, but there were long stretches when there wasn't much to discuss.

At one point, we had high hopes that the Justice Department would drop the charges. My dad had hired a lawyer named Bill Coleman, a former U.S. transportation secretary, to press his case at Justice. Coleman made great progress and was convinced that the charges would be dropped. But Ewing was determined—he wanted my dad. The agony continued.

The first trial finally took place in 1990. It lasted two months. My father's new legal team, led by Bill McDaniels and Ellen Huvelle of Williams and Connolly, was brilliant. I vividly recall watching McDaniels undercut witness after witness. He was so good that at times I forgot how serious the outcome of the trial was for my family. I was thankful that he and Ellen were on our side.

The prosecution's key witnesses were employees of United American Bank. On the stand, they all said something along the lines of, "We were told to disburse these funds to Harold Ford with no paperwork, no questions, and no expectations for him to pay the bank back."

During his cross-examination, McDaniels began by asking, "You don't recall any documentation, and Harold Ford never made payments on these loans?"

"No."

"You were just told to do this without documenting it?"

"Yes, no documentation was presented."

"None at all?"

"No."

McDaniels would then produce a document and say, "Do you recognize this document?"

"Yes, I do."

"Would you just read to the jury what the letterhead is on the document? What's the stationery?"

"United American Bank."

"Who signed it?"

"Me."

"Can you read what the title is?"

"Ford Loan Documents."

"Could you read the first paragraph?"

And the witnesses would read something that refuted their earlier testimony.

As the trial unfolded, the prosecutors led the press and my dad's lawyers to believe that they had yet to produce their star witness, C. H. Butcher. He was supposedly going to seal the prosecution's case: *You better believe we bribed Harold Ford. He took every dime and gave us everything we wanted*, he was supposed to say.

C. H. Butcher never testified. My belief was that he couldn't and wouldn't lie about my father. When C. H. didn't testify, the prosecution rested. My dad's lawyer didn't think the prosecution had proved their case, but my dad wanted to take the stand and proclaim his innocence. McDaniels advised him not to. "There's no need for you to take the stand. If you do, you're going to open yourself up to a lot of questions that could prove embarrassing. We have enough to prevail," McDaniels said.

My dad said, "It doesn't matter. I want to take the stand. They need to hear the truth from my own mouth." Ultimately my dad took his lawyers' advice and didn't take the stand.

The jury deliberated for a little less than a day. As we sat in the courtroom waiting for the foreman to read the verdicts, I was nervous. "On the first count," the foreman said, with uncertain syntax, "we the jury find eight for not guilty, four for guilty. On the second count, we the jury—"

"Objection, Your Honor! Objection!" bellowed the assistant U.S. attorney. McDaniels stood to object as well. The jury had completely misunderstood the judge's instructions for a unanimous verdict.

"That was not a unanimous verdict you were reading," the judge said.

The foreman said that the jurors believed they had followed the judge's instructions, and the judge explained the difference between a unanimous verdict and a majority verdict. Ewing immediately moved for a mistrial, saying the misunderstood instructions had prejudiced the government's case. The prosecution knew that my father was likely to be found innocent if the jury continued to deliberate. We believed that, too.

Ewing feared that. His reputation as a U.S. attorney revolved around getting my dad.

The judge granted the U.S. attorney's motion for a mistrial—against the wishes of my dad and his lawyers. It was a big surprise, actually, because the trial had lasted for several weeks after almost eight years of investigating. I would have thought that the judge would have wanted closure for everyone involved. I was wrong.

My dad's second trial was three years later. Some things had changed. Clinton was now the president. Ewing had been replaced with an even more conservative prosecutor named Ed Bryant.

Ed Bryant was a Tennessee political organizer for Pat Robertson's presidential campaign in 1988. He was a true conservative believer. He also had political aspirations himself. The second trial had another unique feature. The jury was going to be bused into Memphis from Jackson, Tennessee, another part of the Western District of Tennessee, because the U.S. attorney convinced the judge that the government couldn't get a fair trial in Memphis.

How, my dad's lawyers argued, could the government possibly argue that it couldn't get a fair trial? It had spent nearly ten years and $20 million on the case. A trial with a jury from Jackson to decide a man's fate in Memphis seemed to me to violate the principle of being judged by one's peers. But the prosecutors had accomplished their primary goal—to purge the jury of any blacks. The jury pool from Jackson would be predominantly white. The prosecutors would exercise all of their strikes—the removal of jury candidates "just because"—against black jury pool members, thereby reducing to almost zero the number of black jurors.

I could see how painful it was for my father to have to go through the trial a second time. I decided to move to Memphis for the duration of the trial. My dad hadn't asked me to be there; I decided I needed to be there. I was working for Commerce Secretary Ron Brown, and when I told him I needed to take a leave of absence, he said, "I understand. Go on down there, support your father in this case, and then get back to work." The Browns and Fords were neighbors and good friends. Secretary Brown, whose kids are like family, was like an uncle to me.

The lawyers arrived in Memphis about a week before the trial. My dad and I moved into a hotel for the duration of the trial. The lawyers stayed at our home. It was cheaper for my dad to do it that way.

During jury selection, we would leave the hotel at about six in the morning. We'd meet Bill and my dad's other lawyer, Tom Patton, at the house. Ellen Huvelle was now a judge in D.C.; Tom took over for her. Our friend Walter Bailey rented us his very comfortable RV with a driver for the hour and a half ride to Jackson each morning.

My dad had been caricatured by the Memphis press over the years as a fiery black politician. The prosecution knew that to convict my dad, they needed that portrait to dominate the psyche of potential jurors. It was the prosecution's firm conviction, I believed, that my dad was disliked by rural whites to such an extent that these rural whites would convict him based on that alone, and any blacks who happened to make it onto the jury would feel pressured by the whites to convict.

Unsurprisingly, the prosecutors tried to stack the jury with the most conservative people they could find.

My dad's lawyers said to potential jurors, "You're going to hear a lot of accusations. Do you think you will be able to separate fact from fiction? If the prosecutor says something that really offends you, will you give me an opportunity to show you that what he said wasn't true? Or that it may have happened, and it should offend you, but that my client didn't do it?"

You could see the doubt about my father evidenced by the jurors' facial expressions. Their expressions seemed to say, "Yeah, right." They would say, "You're telling me that if he says something about your client and you say it's not true, I'm supposed to believe you instead of him?"

I was listening to this and thinking, "Man, this is going to be tough."

It was hard for me to comprehend how the Memphis press could fail to recognize the magnitude of this travesty. It was even harder for me to comprehend how the national press could ignore what was happening in Tennessee in 1993. At that moment, I assumed control of the press operation for my dad. I started making calls and writing press releases. I thought that if a national newspaper did a story on the jury selection, it might spark outrage in Washington. Every afternoon, I sent press releases to the *Washington Post, USA Today, Newsweek, Time,* and the *New York Times.* After what seemed like weeks of trying—it was actually days—a syndicated columnist named DeWayne Wickham called me. He worked for Gannett, so his columns often appeared in *USA Today*. I can't tell you how good it felt to get his call that midweek afternoon. I was sitting in Jackson, in the law offices of our local counsel during a courtroom break.

"Are you serious?" Wickham asked me. "This is actually happening in 1993? If what you're telling me is even halfway true, this is a farce." He was offended and amused.

"I'm serious, but you can help change the situation by bringing national attention to it," I said, sounding like the excited twenty-two-year-old I was. "This hasn't happened since the sixties. You have an African American on trial and the prosecution is being allowed to select and then bus in a racially purged jury. I'd like you to talk to my father for a few minutes if you can."

My dad talked to Wickham and handed me back the phone. "Good job!" he whispered.

"I'm going to write my next column about this," Wickham said. "It'll be out in two days in *USA Today* and then in dozens of newspapers across the country. Send me whatever you have, and if I need anything else, I'll ring you back." Just before hanging up the phone, he said, "I still can't believe this."

Wickham wrote his column, but his editors didn't run it. They didn't think the story deserved national attention. Wickham fought them until they finally ran it. ("I'm going to get this in the paper—I promise you," he told me. "I'm pissed off about it now, and I'm going to show the same kind of energy and persistence that you are.")

My dad was a member of the Congressional Black Caucus (CBC), and he and the other caucus members happened to be at the White House for a meeting with the president the morning that Wickham's column ran. It was unclear how many White House officials read the story; no one mentioned it. But several CBC members had pointed it out to administration staffers that morning. My dad was asked about Wickham's column at the press gaggle. His response: "The piece paints an honest portrait of what's happening." A few weeks before, CBC members had hand-delivered a letter to the Department of Justice asking for a review of the judge's jury-selection decision. They argued that my father deserved a trial not just in Memphis, but with a Memphis jury. Busing in a racially cleansed jury from ninety miles away for the trial of a United States congressman, they wrote, was the way justice was delivered in the fifties and sixties—but not in the nineties.

Soon afterward, the *Washington Post* editorialized about the improper jury-selection process, and the *New York Times* soon followed.

After the *USA Today* story appeared, the acting attorney general, Stuart Gerson, began looking into the particulars of the case. Gerson was a Republican holdover. Clinton had not gotten his attorney general confirmed yet, so Gerson was acting AG. Gerson's inquiry concluded with him asking the U.S. attorneys in Memphis to ask the judge to not seat the jury because of the appearance of unfairness. He noted the composition of the jury and the regional demographics—a jury that was 8 percent black being bused into a city that was 60 percent black—and said this could jeopardize the credibility of the case.

We had learned from the White House that Gerson would be asking for a new jury shortly before he issued his statement. I'll never forget sitting in my father's office with his lawyers and my mother when we got the call. It was evening, and my dad was sitting in his big desk chair when the call came in. He answered the phone—as always, he had the phone on the credenza behind his desk. He listened, then turned around to face us, with his arm raised and flashing a smile. We had gotten Justice's attention on the issue of unfair jury selection.

"They're going to weigh in tomorrow," he said after he hung up, "and ask to have jury selection redone." We were euphoric. We assumed that the U.S. attorney would follow the instructions of the acting attorney general.

But when Ed Bryant got Gerson's instructions to make this motion of the court, he quit. He actually quit! Bryant had always planned to run for Congress in 1994, in the same district that had supplied the jury pool, and he decided to use the case to launch his campaign. He issued his own statement, to the effect of, "The Clinton administration has come in here and sided with Harold Ford. They are interfering in this investigation and trying to manipulate the makeup of the jury. This is politics," Bryant said. Gerson defended his decision and reminded Bryant that he, Gerson, was a Republican, too. Nonetheless, Bryant was off and running for Congress, and he won in 1994—a banner year for Republicans.

With Bryant gone, his assistant U.S. attorney, Dan Clancy, was now in charge. But Clancy refused to make the Justice Department's argument. Ultimately, Gerson sent a Justice Department lawyer from Washington down to make the argument before the court—we had a different judge for the second trial.

At the hearing, Clancy got up and said, "We want to make it clear that we don't agree with the Department of Justice, Your Honor."

The lawyer from the Justice Department argued Gerson's decision. She gave a solid but unspectacular performance—A for effort though. She argued appearance and nothing else. The judge said, "If you don't think this jury is unfit, we're moving on. I don't care if you don't like the appearances here. I'm not going to unseat them. Both sides had strikes, and everybody exercised those strikes fully and appropriately. I'm going to move on. The trial will start."

The whole sequence of events was unbelievable. After the judge's decision that the jury should be seated, my father began to have chest pains. He was hospitalized for a few days; fortunately he was just dehydrated. The start of the trial was delayed a few days. The next few weeks would be among the most challenging—and rewarding—of my life.

THE EVENING NEWS in Memphis began and ended with coverage of the trial.

Reporters followed us everywhere we went. All the local TV affiliates—ABC, NBC, CBS, and Fox—covered the trial closely. My dad's office was in the same federal building as the courthouse, and the local nightly news opened with a shot of his office each night of the trial.

I was running press, and it was a full-time job. I was

constantly making calls and issuing releases to correct the press. Most of the reporters didn't have any legal background and didn't understand what was happening. They often missed big moments. They might stay for the prosecution's direct examination but leave before the cross-examination. On several occasions, the local TV news would lead with false but attention-grabbing headlines: "Witness says Ford never paid on loan. Details at 5:00." My dad and I were engaged in a constant discussion about how to counter negative portrayals in the media. We understood that the trial was a political event as much as a legal one. It reminded me of the press coverage the Black Student League often got at Penn from the student newspaper.

My dad had been my best friend since I was thirteen or fourteen, but the trial brought us closer in ways that few things can. It is stress I would not wish on anyone, but it did strengthen the bond between my dad and me. We spent two and a half months together nonstop. For eighteen hours a day, we were either in each other's presence or in adjacent rooms. Any press photo he was in, I was in. Wherever he went, I went with him.

Throughout the trial, my dad inspired me. He never allowed himself to show weakness. He was exhausted at times, but he was never dejected. He wore the same suit for the duration of the trial. He never stopped believing that he would come through it. Friends and political allies were distancing themselves from him or abandoning him, but he remained focused and resolute. He showed a strength of character and temperament that I appreciate more and more the older I get.

At some point, the press began speculating about the implications of my involvement in the trial. I was described as my father's closest confidant, and commentators began suggesting that I was a likely successor one day to my dad in Congress. But I was only twenty-two years old, and all I wanted was for my dad to be cleared of all of this.

THE TRIAL ITSELF was almost anticlimactic. The prosecution tried the same case it had tried before—no new materials. It was increasingly obvious that the prosecution's strategy was to change the composition of the jury. Beyond that, the prosecutors had nothing new. They brought the same witnesses they had relied on in the first trial, and McDaniels undercut them all again.

My dad's lawyers scheduled only a few witnesses, including former Memphis mayor Wyatt Chandler. Chandler wasn't called in the first trial. As mayor, Chandler would have had to oversee the construction of the Mud Island bridge, the bridge my dad allegedly arranged federal funding for in exchange for the Butchers' money. Chandler would have known of any illegal activity. My father and he had always been political adversaries. It was a surprise that the prosecutors didn't call Chandler.

A local judge in 1993, Chandler was folksy, very relaxed, and colloquial on the stand. "I seen all this stuff they're accusing Harold Ford of," he said in response to one of McDaniels's questions, "and I had to come and defend him. I don't really like him, and I sure never liked his politics, but I don't like seeing somebody accused of doing something he didn't do. I was the mayor of this town, and I was making the decisions about how the money for the Mud Island bridge got spent. Harold Ford had nothing to do with it. He never called me on the phone. He never sent me a letter. If he had, I would have ignored it because I tried not to pay any attention to him. We fought like cats and dogs."

When the prosecution cross-examined him, he said, unprompted, "I'm surprised you-all didn't call me—I was the mayor." People in the courtroom, especially the jurors, smiled. Chandler's drawl appealed to the jurors. Chandler was a legendary political figure in Memphis and west Tennessee, so all the jurors knew him or knew of him. The prosecution tried to suggest that Chandler was testifying to curry favor with my dad, because he wanted my dad's support in his reelection bid.

"Harold Ford's still a pretty powerful politician, isn't he?" the prosecutor asked him.

"Young man," Chandler said, "let me simmer you down right now. I know where you're going with this line of questioning, and I didn't want to make news right here. I wanted to do it in a more dignified way, but you just forced me to. I'm not going to seek reelection next year. This is my last term. And frankly, if I was seeking reelection, I wouldn't want Harold Ford's support. I came here today because I know he didn't do anything. Now, he may have done other bad things, but what you're accusing him of, he didn't do."

The jurors laughed. People in the courtroom were chuckling. The prosecutor was desperate.

The prosecution couldn't undo the damage Chandler did

to their case, and the big debate within my dad's team that evening became whether or not my dad would take the stand. My dad insisted on it, but his lawyers were adamantly opposed again for the same reasons as in the first trial. The prosecution's case was even weaker in the second trial, McDaniels argued. McDaniels reminded my father that he could be forced to explain some embarrassing things. McDaniels also noted that the prosecution had worked hard to select jurors with very modest incomes who might be suspicious of politicians with a big home and a nice car.

I'll never forget my dad saying, "The jury needs to hear me say I'm innocent of these charges." My dad was going to testify. He would not be talked out of it. I agreed with him.

McDaniels acknowledged that in the end it was not up to him. "This is your life," he said, "and ultimately it's your decision."

The next morning, my father took the stand, and it was high drama. The prosecutors wanted to establish the relationship between one of the codefendants in the trial, Karl Schledwitz, and my dad. They believed that Karl and my dad met during the Butcher campaigns. In fact, the prosecution was wrong.

"You didn't meet him in a political context with the Butchers?"

My dad said, "No," and continued, "I met him—" The prosecutor objected, "Your Honor, I think he's answered the question." My dad said, "Your Honor, he asked me a question, and I'm trying to answer it fully. It isn't as simple as, 'How do you know him?' He made it sound in this trial as if Karl and I met in the course of a crime, which never happened. So let me explain this fully. He's done a lot of talking. This is the first time I've had a chance to answer the U.S. attorney in ten years."

The judge agreed with my dad. My dad described meeting Schledwitz, who had been president of the student body at the University of Tennessee and had gone to Nashville to complain about slum landlords on campus. Schledwitz had told my dad that students were being overcharged for rent, which prompted my dad to sponsor a bill on behalf of University of Tennessee students to stop these abusive practices. My dad described all of this in detail. He was in fine form. The nervousness that gripped him at the start of the cross-examination had dissolved. To the chagrin of the prosecution, the jury was listening closely. My dad was looking at them as he answered the questions. I knew they believed him, because he was telling the truth. Again, he was having a conversation with people, but he was the only one talking.

When we got home that evening, Tom Patten jubilantly expressed, "Let me tell you something. I was sitting here last night worried as hell about you testifying. I went to bed worried as hell about you testifying. I awakened worried." Tom was excited and smiling now.

"Harold, when they asked you that first question," he said, "I sat there and wondered, 'How is he going to answer that?' And I've never heard a more brilliant answer. You hit him hard. You popped him. And then he asked you another question and you hit him again. And then another question, and another hit."

McDaniels had a big smile on his face as he watched Tom. "I can't believe this," Tom said. "It's over. If tomorrow you do what you did today, it's over." My dad's lawyers had agonized for a week over his testimony. To say they were pleased is an understatement. We were all pleased, but we knew it wasn't over yet.

In his closing, McDaniels answered every charge and dispensed with every question the prosecution raised:

> Let me remind you of what I said at the beginning. There would be a number of allegations made about Harold Ford by the prosecution. Not one of them is true. Let me repeat, every one of them has been proven untrue by the evidence. The right outcome in this trial is an acquittal on all of the charges brought against Harold Ford. The prosecution's case has been entirely based on innuendo and lies. These charges are sensational in nature. They are designed in part to provoke emotional reactions from you, but you have a duty to separate fact from fiction, and you can do that by looking at the abundance of evidence we have presented proving Harold Ford's innocence.

McDaniels then went through all of the charges individually and pointed to the evidence that refuted the charge, so that when the jurors retreated to deliberate, each would know exactly where to find the exonerating evidence—which exhibits to look for or which documents to reference. "I submit to you that this is a bribery case unique in the annals of time. Even though we know this matter has been investigated since at least as early as 1982 with, among other devices, secretly recorded telephone conversations, there has been no evidence of any action by the elected public official Harold Ford to favor improperly the Butchers in exchange for loans. No phone call, no letter, no meeting, no lobbying effort, no legislation . . . when the government asks you the jury to strip the office of an elected public official by convicting him of a crime for selling his office, it must produce evidence to sustain that charge. It has not done so here," said McDaniels.

McDaniels was at his best—he gave the jurors the Cliffs-Notes on where to look.

In their closing, the prosecution did exactly what McDaniels predicted. They used theatrics to compensate for a breathtaking lack of evidence. As I sat and listened to the assistant U.S. attorney walk the jury through the charges, I couldn't help but think how long this had gone on, how financially costly this episode was, and, most important, the depth of personal pain it had inflicted on my dad, my mom, my brothers, and me over ten years. I wanted to win this thing, put it behind us and move on.

Listening to McDaniels, Wyatt Chandler, and my dad reinforced this, and it was hard to see how the jury could vote to convict. I wanted to be angry—and part of me really was—but more than anything I wanted my dad to be cleared of all of the charges. My dad had friends who had abandoned him during this time. Some politicians, including the mayor, and most of the press had written my dad's political obituary many times. After hearing the evidence, I was encouraged but I couldn't be certain until the jury returned an acquittal on each of the charges.

Finally, the prosecutor ended his closing argument and the matter was turned over to the jury.

It was Wednesday afternoon when it all finished. My dad, the legal team, and the rest of us retreated to his office for a late lunch. No one knew how long the jury would deliberate. We waited all day Thursday with no word from the court. I started to worry that the jury was undecided on some of the charges. I feared that the jury might deliver a mixed verdict—some acquittals and some convictions. We went to the hotel Thursday night as a family not knowing the outcome.

Midmorning on Friday—Good Friday—we made our way to my dad's office on the third floor in the federal building. The courtroom was a few floors above us. Almost immediately, the phones began to ring in my dad's office. He was getting calls from friends all across the city, including some in the Memphis police and fire departments. They were telling him that all off-duty police in the city and many off-duty firemen were being called back to work. That was all the information they had, but they assumed it had something to do with the trial. We noticed that U.S. Marshals were arriving at the federal building in buses. There were soon twice as many U.S. Marshals near the courtroom.

I was thinking that the jury was going to convict. Word had somehow gotten out, and the city was bracing for demonstrations and possibly riots. The case, after all, had received saturation coverage. The town was caught up in it. The mayor had openly criticized my dad during the trial. Some of his allies had publicly broken with him. But many of my father's constituents considered the trial a sham. They never stopped believing in him, and to see that loyalty was amazing. The people who showed up every morning for the trial were the very constituents my dad had helped with a utility bill, a social security check, or a housing problem. The press would ask why they were there, and they would say things like, "Because I'll never forget the things he did for me and my community, and I don't believe anything the prosecutors are saying. I know Harold Ford. That's not the kind of person he is."

As we were processing these reports about the increased police and U.S. Marshals' presence at the building, my dad remained as calm as he could. I can only imagine what he was feeling. All of a sudden the phone rang again. It was the court— the jury had reached a verdict. My dad looked over at McDaniels. "What does it mean that it took almost two days?" my dad asked. "Harold, don't read anything into it—we're going to go upstairs and learn that you've been acquitted of all charges," McDaniels said. "As I've told you, I've sat through days of jury deliberations and been gratified by the results."

We got ourselves ready and walked upstairs to the courtroom. I didn't say anything to my dad. He was very calm. He said to McDaniels, "I feel good about this." McDaniels said, "I feel good about it, too, Harold. We did everything we could."

We hadn't been sitting in the courtroom long when the jury came in. The forewoman got up. She was a small woman from just outside Jackson.

"On the first charge," she said, "we find the defendant, Harold Ford, not guilty. On the second charge, we find the defendant, Harold Ford, not guilty . . ." Once she got through the first three charges, we knew he would be found innocent of the last nine, because they were all either codependent charges or multiple counts of the same crime.

I will never forget the image of the forewoman standing there saying, "Not guilty." When I heard those words, it was like the start of a new life.

There were expressions of jubilation even before the forewoman finished reading the verdict. The judge had to tell everybody to be quiet. I couldn't move. Shock and relief were all I felt. Watching someone you love—a parent, a sibling, a spouse—sit in a courtroom with their life hanging in the balance is a harrowing and maturing experience. Once you've been through it, it becomes hard to get too nervous in any situation. I imagine that during the birth of my first child I might experience a greater joy. But the reading of that verdict was a joy I'll never forget.

In the courtroom, after the verdict had been read completely, my father sat quietly for a few moments. My aunts and uncles and cousins were all reaching for his hands. My mom and my brothers and I were sitting behind him, and he leaned back and hugged and kissed us. Everybody was crying. My dad, who had never once cried during either trial, had tears in his eyes. He turned to the members of the jury and silently nodded "Thank you" to each one.

KINDERGARTEN
CONGRESSMAN

DESPITE MY FATHER'S ELEVEN TERMS IN CONGRESS, I began my first congressional campaign with little money and little credibility. When I formally announced in mid-April 1996, I was only twenty-five years old and still in my final semester of law school at the University of Michigan. The political and press establishment in the Ninth Congressional District, which considered me unprepared and presumptuous, was actively hostile to my candidacy.

I graduated from law school on my birthday, Saturday, May 11, 1996, and flew home to Memphis afterward. I had set up my campaign headquarters in a large white Victorian home in midtown Memphis. The headquarters was conveniently dubbed "the White House" by my young campaign staff. My staff threw me a birthday/graduation party that night. The next day, I went to several churches with my family. On Monday, I went in to the campaign headquarters at 6 A.M.—the campaign was now my full-time job.

I had no formal speaking invitations, a nonexistent advertising budget, and no real resources to stage campaign rallies or events. Few savvy political people in the district were taking me seriously.

My staff and I searched the Memphis *Commercial Appeal* for listings of local events that were open to the public. The Optimist Club and Rotary Club listed their meetings, so I would show up and shake hands with attendees before the meetings started. Events honoring public employees were often listed, so I made appearances at going-away parties and retirement dinners for librarians and city bus drivers and postal supervisors. I went to church prayer services, PTA receptions, Neighborhood Watch meetings, and church banquets. I would go to popular breakfast, lunch, and dinner spots and shake hands there, too. The first ten days of the campaign, this is how I spent my time. I was following a long-standing Ford strategy on campaigning. Because of the large-scale press coverage I had gotten, I was recognized by just about everyone. Not afraid to walk into a room full of strangers, I would stand outside the room, hotel, or building where events were taking place and shake every hand I could. "Hi, I'm Harold Ford, Jr.," I would say, "and I'm running for Congress and would appreciate your vote and prayers." Almost everyone shook my hand. I wasn't convinced that voters were sure of me yet, but at least I was demonstrating that I wouldn't shrink from public view in the face of harsh criticism. I wanted voters to know that I didn't fear the fight leading up to an election. I thought: "If I fear a tough campaign, how will voters trust me to fight for them once I get to Washington?" Watching my dad over the years taught me that.

One day early in the campaign, my former elementary

school principal and co–campaign manager, Hattie Jackson, walked into my campaign office at headquarters. Ms. Jackson's involvement as my campaign manager was important to me and my family. She was close to us, and her late husband, H. Ralph Jackson, had been my father's longtime co–campaign chairman until he died several years earlier. Ms. Jackson walked in and said, "Baby, I got you thirty-five speaking engagements. They're graduation speeches." That was welcome news. I almost cried because it was my first set of formal invitations. I assumed they were high school graduations, so I gathered my young volunteers around me and said, "Okay, let's be smart about this. We need to find as many voter registration forms as we can. When I'm giving these speeches, I can't politic from the podium, but I can certainly encourage these kids to register to vote and participate. So let's split up and y'all go out to the libraries around town and the Elections Commission and collect as many forms as you can." Hattie Jackson said, "Baby, wait a second. These graduations are not high school graduations."

I was confused, but I said, "Well, okay. No worries. Get the registration forms anyway. If they're middle school graduations, we'll help their parents and relatives and older siblings fill them out. People may need to change their registration. You never know. My dad has always taught me to be prepared."

Ms. Jackson was still standing there, and she said, "Baby, they're not middle schools either."

I was now really confused. I said, "Ms. Jackson, what are they?"

"Well," she said, "I got you thirty-two kindergarten graduation speeches." The other three were elementary schools.

I thought, "You got me what?" I wanted to be upset about it—these kids were five years old—but I couldn't be because I had no other groups inviting me to speak. I was grateful to Ms. Jackson because she was just trying to help. Kindergartners would have to substitute for audiences of business leaders, women's rights advocates, labor leaders, civil rights activists, and environmental groups.

I embarked on my kindergarten speaking circuit with zeal. I treated the events as if I were speaking to adults, because at least the children's parents and grandparents would probably come. I would stand in front of the kids and tell stories about when I was in kindergarten, like they were, or when I was in elementary school. I liked to tell the story of the one time I was paddled by Ms. Jackson in second grade, at Double Tree Elementary in Memphis. The story went like this: During recess period, all recreation had to take place on the playground and school field. The nearby woods were off-limits. One day, I told the kindergarten graduates, I decided to grab two friends and venture into the woods. Some other kids, mostly older than I, had already gotten caught attempting to play in the woods. I wanted to see if I could get away with it.

This was really the only time during the speech that I held the kindergartners' attention. Early in my speech, many of the kids would fall asleep when I was thanking the teachers, parents, and school staff for inviting me. They would awaken— and their parents were alert, too—when I'd tell this story. Shortly before recess was over, I told them, my friends and I peeked out of the woods to ensure that no teachers were looking, and then ran back onto the playground, where we pretended to be playing with our friends. Recess ended and we returned to class. The kindergartners were locked in now. No sooner had I returned to my seat than Ms. Jackson's voice came over the loud schoolwide PA system asking me to report to the principal's office.

When I got to this part of the story, many of the kids would place their hands over their mouths and make faces and noises—they realized I was in serious trouble with Ms. Jackson. I told them, "You're right, I was in real trouble." I went on to explain how Ms. Jackson paddled me, and then how I was even in more trouble when I got home, because my parents were embarrassed by my actions at school and reprimanded me, too. I wanted to reinforce for these kids that even at a young age, our choices in school impact us and have consequences. They seemed to get it, and I would say, "Now I'd like you to hold your right hands up and repeat after me: 'I promise'—they would respond—'to work hard'—response—'play by the rules'—response—'and keep God first'"—response. Then I turned my attention to the parents, and the kids often dozed off again.

"You've got a role to play," I told the parents. "You need to keep these kids motivated. They're depending on you for that. We punish them when they're wrong, and rightly so, but we must be quick to encourage and congratulate them when they do right." I would urge the parents to spend more time checking homework and test scores, and to commit themselves to attending more school meetings during the next school year, when the kids would reach first grade. Then I would present kindergarten diplomas, shake hands, and take pictures with everyone—including the kitchen and janitorial staff at the school. There were about a hundred people at most of the kindergarten graduations.

I convinced myself that my speech would affect the kids positively. That my words would build on the foundation many of them were getting at school and at home. The political optics didn't concern me much, but it did others. I was enjoying myself and learning. The local press ridiculed me. Articles about me were headlined, "The Kindergarten Wannabe Congressman." The media liked to point out that the graduates I spent the majority of my days speaking to were more than a decade too young to vote. Most reporters stopped covering me two or three speeches in. The press interpreted these graduation speeches as a sign that my campaign was on life support in early June. They couldn't summarily dismiss me, because my father remained a sitting member of Congress, but they didn't give me much of a chance. I figure that every politician can remember a moment when the establishment told them that there was no way they could win.

My dad often drove me from graduation speech to graduation speech, and on the way, we would listen to political talk radio. Callers were lacerating me: I was "too young" and "too inexperienced," and I'd "never had a full-time job." My father was giving me a congressional seat as a gift for graduating from law school, they said. I was completely unqualified and unfit for the job.

I remember saying to my father, "Some of these people are clearly being put up to calling. My opponents are urging them to call in, looking to define me early in the race. Why shouldn't

I do that? Why shouldn't I have people call in to balance it out?" I imagined people calling in and essentially summarizing my résumé: I had worked on Capitol Hill, in the Clinton Administration, and worked for my dad in his local congressional office. I could point to significant accomplishments in college and law school. I had meaningful constituent-service experience.

My dad said, "No need to do that yet. There may come a time when we have to, because it doesn't look like this campaign is going to be particularly civil, but it's too early. Let it rest. The primary's not until August. If people want to call in and say nice things, let them do it, but don't try to manufacture it artificially."

One day we were in the car, driving from one graduation to the next—I had probably completed more than half of my graduation speeches at that point. We had the radio on, and as we were pulling into the driveway of Vollintine Elementary, a caller who identified herself as a grandmother phoned in to the show. She said she had been listening to the show religiously over the last few weeks, and had heard all the harsh words about me.

One of the hosts said, "Well, thank you for listening so regularly. Have you made a decision about who you're going to vote for?"

She said, "Well, you know, I had made my mind up and then I changed it after something that happened yesterday."

The host said, "What happened yesterday?"

She said, "Well, that boy y'all keep talking bad about, Harold Ford, Jr.? I saw him yesterday at my grandbaby's kindergarten graduation."

"Is that right? How bad was he?" the host asked.

"Well, I want you to know that he walked into that school auditorium, got up before those kids, and started speaking, and no sooner did he start speaking than all those kids fell asleep."

Both hosts laughed.

"But that didn't stop him. He kept talking and talking and talking. Talked about how important his education was—the education he got in kindergarten and when he attended elementary school. How it helped him get to where he was and go to college and run for Congress. He said a lot of people were criticizing him but that he wasn't going to be deterred. And he pledged to work hard and urged those kids to work hard, play by the rules, and keep God first, and he told them their parents believed in them." She practically quoted my speech.

"And after he finished talking," she said, "he took pictures with every student and shook their hands and gave them their diplomas. He took pictures with the parents and the grandparents, and he took pictures with the teachers and the principal, and shook hands with everybody. He even went back to the lunchroom and took pictures with all of the staff back in the kitchen. Now, that reminded me of his daddy. That boy is just like his daddy. And if he's like his daddy, I'm going to vote for him for Congress."

The host was dumbfounded. "I have trouble believing that you are going to vote for him just because he went around posing for pictures and shaking hands."

She said, "I'm going to vote for him because he conducts himself just like his daddy. And I want a congressman like that.

You all have him pegged wrong, I think. You should go to one of his speeches."

I looked over at my dad. We were still sitting in the car.

"That's why you stay the course," said my dad as he opened his door to head in to the graduation with me. It was at this moment that a real momentum shift occurred in my favor. I faced hardship and stress throughout the remainder of the campaign, but this was a turning point, and it showed me and the young people around me that we were starting to impact the race in our favor.

Then another grandmother who had heard me speak at a kindergarten graduation called in right after and said more or less the same thing. Then someone else who had heard me called in, and the sentiment spread to more and more listeners. The calls kept coming in. The callers were a mixture of grand-mothers, mothers, and aunts, and my presence at these gradu-ations had made an impression on people: "He spoke at my baby's graduation," "He spoke at my son's graduation," "He spoke at my nephew's graduation," "He spoke at my niece's graduation," and so on. It was as if we had drawn up a script and everyone had delivered their lines perfectly—except that I never could have written a script this good.

The campaign was turning because of efforts that I never thought would yield this kind of momentum. The kindergar-ten graduation speeches were catalysts. They helped decon-struct the portrait that my opponents and the press were trying to draw of me as an out-of-touch congressman's son with no feel for, care about, or understanding of real Memphis issues.

The kindergarten graduation speeches humanized me and connected me with thousands of people across the congressional district. They changed my campaign and political trajectory. Miss Jackson was right again.

The press's nickname for me, "Kindergarten Congressman," became a compliment. Eventually, I became known as the "Education Congressman," a candidate who listened to and learned to understand the needs of kids and educators. I started spending even more time on school campuses. I went to elementary, middle, and high schools. When summer came around, I visited summer camps and spoke there, too. The press was following me again.

This taught me something very valuable: You never know when opportunity is going to spring forth. You never know exactly what a given set of circumstances will produce. But opportunity is everywhere. I never thought the kindergarten graduations would amount to anything. I was wrong. Often, the moment it seems least likely that something positive will emerge, it does. And it did here.

AFTER HIS ACQUITTAL, my father went right back to work in Congress, reclaiming his chairmanship of the Ways and Means Subcommittee and throwing himself into the debate over Clinton's welfare-reform policies. However, I could tell he considered the verdict the start of a new, post-political stage in his life. Even before the trial, I sensed that he didn't want to run again. At forty-seven, he was wearying of Congress. He was frustrated by the carelessness with which the Democrats had wielded power when they were in the majority. The Democratic Party was failing to give positions of authority and influence to talented young congresspeople, and it had stubbornly resisted new ideas and approaches.

During the first semester of my second year in law school, in the fall of 1994, I started commuting home every weekend to work as my father's campaign manager. It was a tough year for congressional Democrats. There was a new depth of personal and professional trust between my dad and me as a result of the trial. I wasn't just invited to sit in on policy and strategy meetings; I was a full partner at the table—his most trusted adviser. Members of the Memphis political and press establishments regarded me as his chief spokesperson because I had served in that role during the trial, and they often came to me when they needed a comment from him or to get a message to him. His political allies also knew that he trusted me.

I didn't fully appreciate it then, but my father was signaling that I was qualified to succeed him in Congress. When he was reelected for the last time, in 1994, few thought he would not run in 1996—it was assumed that he would remain in office for a few more terms, at least—but people in the political establishment were beginning to look at me differently.

In the spring of 1995, my dad, mom, brothers, and I grabbed dinner at a restaurant near Mazza Gallerie in D.C. while I was home for a weekend from law school. As the rest of the family walked to the table, my father said to me, "This is my last term. If you are serious about running, you should start getting ready. Start scheduling time to be in Memphis and begin meeting with key people. I will help, but you must show

the initiative." Many political observers believed that my dad
and I had conspired about when and how I would run. It didn't
happen that way at all. There was a progression, but there was
no grand plan. He told me at a family dinner—on the way to
the table.

The way he did it reminded me of the kind of testing he
usually reserved for those who wanted to win his political support in Memphis. "The seat belongs to the voters," he always
said, "and no one is entitled to it. You earn it by serving or by
proving that you will serve the people. *Titles don't entitle you to
anything.*" My dad had always practiced that, and now he
wanted me to show that I was capable, ready, and willing to
serve the district. He was testing me.

With that in mind, my father chose to announce that he
would not seek reelection a full six weeks before the filing
deadline for the Democratic primary, which was mid-May
1996. If he had waited until the last minute, he would have
kept people out of the race. No one wanted to run against a
popular twenty-two-year incumbent with superb political acu-
men. Many politicians who want their offspring to succeed
them make their decision public just before the filing deadline
in order to hold challengers out of the race. My dad gave potential candidates plenty of time. That opened up the field and
demonstrated that he had confidence that voters would choose
the best candidate—even if that wasn't me. Had he tried to
push people out, it would have made me look weak.

The first thing I did after making my decision, and in retrospect one of the most important, was to begin meeting with
leaders all across the district. This was my father's first piece of

advice. I talked to everyone who might help me and everyone who might oppose me. Thus began the protracted process of establishing my credibility and independence. I took nothing for granted. I didn't expect to inherit my father's relationships or reputation, and I had to communicate that to the district's political leaders. While my father offered advice about whom to reach out to, he never attended a meeting with me or made preliminary calls on my behalf.

Nor did he solicit feedback from the people I was meeting with, although he often heard from them. Without making a deliberate effort to do so, he evaluated my conduct. He was alert to signs of self-entitlement and to any failure to conduct myself with sufficient gravity and humility, and I knew better than to disappoint him.

My father's contact list included adversaries as well as allies. "You go see everybody on that list—everybody. If you want to do it like I did, you go see everybody, regardless of the nature of their relationship with me, and treat everybody with respect." I went down the list, excluding no one. It ended up being an encompassing listening tour across the district. It was the summer of 1995. I split my summer between Washington and Memphis law firms—Patton Boggs in D.C. during the first half and Hanover Walsh Jalenak & Blair in Memphis for the second. My first day on the job in Memphis I went to lunch with one of the named partners, and one of the best and most respected lawyers in town—Jimmy Jalenak—and shared with him that my long-term plan was to run for Congress.

"When are you thinking about making this run?" Jimmy asked.

"Next year," I said.

He looked back down at his plate of meat and continued eating. I couldn't read him. Then he said, "Count me in. I want to help." And he did. To date, the strategy sessions at Uncle Jimmy's house were the most fun because he gave great advice. And his wife, Natalie, made the best chicken salad.

I spent the remainder of the summer doing my work at the firm by day and working at my family's funeral home on selected evenings—mainly when there were funerals. I ate lunch at popular spots in town and after work would do district events with my father in the evening. I didn't openly talk about running for office, and neither did my dad.

It would be naïve and disingenuous of me to say that my name and connections were not enormously helpful. They were. But it was becoming clear that I would be held to a higher standard. There would be no simple transfer of loyalty and commitment from my father's supporters to me. There was a credibility threshold I had to cross, and I had to cross it alone.

ONCE MY FINAL year of law school started back up in September 1995, I had to develop a class schedule to accommodate my travel to Memphis once a week. So I did. My last class would end at noon on Wednesdays. That gave me time to catch a 3:00 P.M. Northwest flight out of Detroit to Memphis. Conveniently, there was a late Sunday return flight, which would get me back to Ann Arbor in time for Monday morning classes.

◆　　　◆

IT WAS THE week after the Million Man March in Washington, D.C. The march, organized by Minister Louis Farrakhan, took place October 16, 1995, on the steps of the U.S. capitol. My friend Jerry Fanion had been at the march in Washington. I told Jerry that I was giving serious thought to running for Congress if my dad didn't run, and I asked him if he wouldn't mind traveling around the district with me and accompanying me to meetings. He agreed to do it. Jerry knew everyone—the people with the biggest and most prestigious titles, and the equally important but uncredentialed people as well.

In late October, the first official meeting I set up as I started this congressional exploration was with the late Pastor Kenneth Whalum, Sr., at his church, Olivet Baptist. The press and political establishment were now aware that my dad was seriously considering not running. There had been much speculation about Reverend Whalum running for Congress. He would have been a formidable opponent. Growing up, I had spent time in his church because my father was a member there. My brothers and I regularly split time among Olivet, the Temple of Deliverance (pastored by Bishop G. E. Patterson), and other churches where my dad spoke. We later joined Mt. Moriah-East Baptist Church as a family.

I met with Reverend Whalum in his private office. Sitting across the table from him, I was more honored and humbled than nervous. I had always admired him for his independent thinking and his ministry. My intent was not necessarily to discern his interest in running. I was more interested in assuring him of my respect and admiration of him, and in conveying the seriousness with which I was approaching the race and the duties of being a congressman. In fact, I felt like he was interviewing me, and I wanted him to leave the meeting believing that I was ready to be a strong candidate and a good congressman. And, on another level, I wanted him to know that I would be a worthy competitor if he decided to run. I said:

> Pastor, I've given a lot of thought to this, and I want to be candid with you. If my father does not run (I wasn't going to give anything away before the official announcement), I have an ambitious plan for the next several months. I'll be traveling across the district, meeting with leaders like yourself, talking to as many people as I can, and asking for advice and ultimately support if my dad doesn't run. I wanted to let you know my plans. I've read that you're thinking about running, and I assume you've given it a lot of thought, as I have, and you are serious about it, as I am. If we both run, I hope we have a civil race, an honest race, and a spirited race, and, dare I say it, even a fun race. And if you don't run, I'd like to come back and ask for your support and advice throughout the campaign.

Pastor Whalum said, "Young man, listen to me. I'm not going to run. I'm getting of an age where flying back and forth to Washington every week just doesn't appeal to me."

"Well, Reverend," I said, "it does to me."

"I want you to know, first of all, that I've known you since you were a boy, and I think you've become a good man. But there will be many awful things said about you personally," he told me. "People will paint you as an undeserving beneficiary of your father's hard work. You will inherit his friends and enemies. Are you ready for that?"

"I believe so, sir."

He recommended that I see his son, who had also surfaced as a potential candidate. Additionally, his son was emerging as a powerful pastor in his own right. Reverend Whalum, Sr., ended up not running and supported me. Kenneth Jr. didn't run, but he supported one of my opponents in the primary.

Soon I was doing six or seven meetings a day. The conversations evolved and matured. The meetings—which were increasingly like job interviews—helped me to better understand the needs of people and neighborhoods throughout the district. Educators and small-business people were able to help me understand their respective areas of expertise, but I made a point of asking them questions about issues like crime and health care in their neighborhoods as well, because I believed that a teacher's take on crime might be just as useful as that of a law enforcement professional in finding real answers, and two perspectives are more instructive than one. I asked doctors and pastors to tell me about the state of education and economic development in their neighborhoods. It proved to be a valuable technique.

People had nothing but positive things to say about my father. They very openly expressed their admiration for his leadership and service. They were understandably wary of pledging support for me at such an early stage, but many said,

"If I do support you, I would want to make sure that you and I had the same relationship your dad and I have." Naturally I assured them that that would be the case, and I demonstrated it with follow-up meetings. "Follow-up" was key. I could hear my dad's voice in my head.

Although I wasn't campaigning, I wanted to show my seriousness and sincerity, so I visited the same churches, schools, fire and police stations, restaurants, and small businesses multiple times. Soon after I started making these rounds, opposition got louder. Memphis's mayor, Willie Herenton, led the opposition.

His objection to my candidacy was inspired by one thing: He wanted full control of the Memphis political landscape. My dad's retirement from Congress presented Herenton with a chance to consolidate political power, he believed. If I won, it would threaten his plan. I wasn't fond of Herenton personally because of how he treated my dad during his trial. He betrayed us. I even believed that Herenton and some of his political team were responsible for a horrible Christmas Eve morning in 1995.

On December 23 of that year, I attended Herenton's Christmas party. It was a black-tie affair held at the convention center in downtown Memphis. I left the party at around 10:30 P.M. with Jerry Freeman, a University of Michigan classmate, and Jerry Fanion. My dad was in his robe when we got home. We all sat down with my dad at the kitchen table and talked a while about the day and the event, and then Jerry Fanion decided to head home. All of the time Fanion spent helping me obviously took time from his family life. His wife, Jackie, was the most understanding wife and mom in Memphis. Jerry Freeman and I decided to get a late meal at an all-night restaurant about a mile from my dad's house.

As Freeman and I were pulling out of the driveway, we noticed that Fanion was sitting in his truck on the other side of the street with his blinkers on. Thinking that something was wrong with his truck, I pulled over and asked what was going on.

"I just saw two guys running through your dad's front yard," he said. "One of them was carrying a camera." In Fanion's day job, he was a deputy sheriff. "You-all go back in the house and let your dad know," he said and then walked across the street to question them.

I turned my car around and drove back to my dad's house. We lived in a complex of town houses about 150 feet from the road, with a big gated yard in front. Adjacent to the complex was the Lipman School, and these two guys had parked in the school's parking lot.

"Dad, there are men with TV cameras outside," I said as we walked into the house.

"What are you talking about?" he asked loudly from his bedroom.

"I don't know what's going on," I said, "but Jerry Fanion is out there with them right now. They're parked over in the Lipman School parking lot, and Fanion can't get them to answer any questions about why they are outside."

We all walked to the front door. I could tell my dad was

angry. By now it was midnight. My dad, Jerry Freeman, and I walked over to the parking lot where the TV crew was parked. It was about 100 yards from the house.

"What are y'all doing in front of my home on Christmas Eve?" my dad yelled into the closed passenger-side window, where the guy with the camera was sitting. The driver was on his cell phone, and neither of them would lower his window or open the doors. The car was running. After a few attempts, my dad called the local NBC affiliate and asked them to come out and report on the fact that reporters from the local CBS affiliate had trespassed on his property and now wouldn't explain what they were doing. He also phoned and left a message for the president of the CBS affiliate to ask why his station had sent two men to stake out his property. I was still dressed in my tux, without the tie. I was as confused as my dad was.

Eventually, my dad reached the CBS president, who said that he was unaware of any crew being assigned to our house, but would find out what was going on. The camera crew finally drove off; my dad and I returned to the house. It was about 1:30 A.M. Fanion and Freeman went home. The president phoned back twenty minutes later with more information: They were following a lead on me. "What?" my dad said into the phone. The president told him that the affiliate had heard that I had been involved in a car accident and was following up on the story. While my dad was on the phone with the CBS affiliate, we received another call on another line from a good family friend, the late Charlie Regan. When I answered the phone, Charlie said, "Harold Jr., how are you?"

"I'm fine, sir," I answered.

"You sure?" he asked cryptically. "Let me speak to your dad." I called my dad over, and he came to the kitchen and took the phone.

"Harold Jr. is fine," my dad said. "What are you talking about, 'Is he badly injured?'"

"I just got a call from some friends who were hit by a drunk driver on the interstate, and they said Channel 3 [the CBS affiliate] is outside their house right now," Charlie continued. He was on speakerphone now. "The Channel 3 reporters are saying that the person who hit them was Harold Jr., but my friends never saw him because the ambulance came so quickly."

This was unbelievable. The reporters were insisting that it was me, and they wanted the crash victims, Charlie's friends, to go on camera and say that they'd been hit by me and that I was drunk.

"Neither the police nor the hospital will provide any information on Harold Jr.'s involvement," Charlie continued. "Channel 3 is telling my friends that you pulled strings to get Harold Jr. out of jail after he was released from the trauma unit at the regional medical center."

It became clear. Channel 3 was at my house looking to cover a cover-up.

My dad and I were listening to our family friend on the phone and looking at each other in disbelief. I hadn't been drinking nor had I been in any accident. We never learned who was behind this manufactured story. I suspected then that it was Herenton, with some help from the CBS affiliate.

But I put aside my personal feelings and went to see him in early 1996 even after it was clear that he was recruiting candidates to run for the congressional seat against me. His most prominent and high-profile recruit was the speaker pro tem of the Tennessee House of Representatives, Lois DeBerry. She was—and remains—a longtime friend of my family. I have known her all my life. She rebuffed Herenton, and so did several others.

Initially it wasn't my strength as a potential candidate that was scaring off the challengers. It was the strength of my dad's record in the district that concerned potential candidates. And interestingly my dad didn't threaten anyone. Actually, it was the opposite. My dad encouraged candidates who wanted to run, to run. There was one young county commissioner who indicated publicly that he wanted to run for Congress. He was critical of me and my father, calling my candidacy nepotism at its worst. But it became clear that he was really interested in a different political office—the mayor's office. He thought he should have been elected mayor five years earlier. He blamed my father for not selecting him instead of Herenton to run as the "people's" candidate in 1991. The people's candidate was the result of a convention of black leaders organized by community leaders to pick one black candidate for the mayor's race in 1991. Memphis had never elected a black mayor. Many people wanted my dad to run, but he didn't want to. Instead he influenced the ultimate selection of Herenton as the candidate.

So one Saturday afternoon, this county commissioner met my dad and me to discuss his future political plans. I didn't know what to expect. But I did know that the county commissioner expected something in return if he decided not to run for Congress. Right after the meeting started, the commissioner expected my father to acknowledge that a deal was on the table and to enter smoothly into the discussion. My father was very calm and cordial and acted as if he had no idea why the meeting had been set up. My dad just made casual conversation. "So, how can I help you?" he finally asked.

"Well, what I was thinking—you've probably seen the press," the commissioner said.

"I see a lot of press," my dad said. "I've read things about my son, about me, about this race. Tell me what you're thinking. I'd like to hear what's on your mind."

"Look, I don't really want to run for Congress. I want to run for mayor in three years, but I'm unclear about what you [my dad] will decide to do. Have you made a decision about the mayor's race?" asked the commissioner.

"Let me get this straight," my dad said. "You want me to agree to support you in a race that's three years away so that you won't run in a congressional race today because you think that will give my son an advantage?" My dad cut to the chase.

"Well, that's right," he said. "What I'm saying is, I think Harold Jr. deserves a chance to run without me being in the race."

"I'm not in the business of making political deals like that," my dad said. And then he continued:

I don't know what you've heard, but that's not what I do. All Harold Jr. deserves is a chance to run for Congress. He doesn't deserve any special advantage. The voters will make a determination. So my advice for you is pretty simple. If you want to run for mayor, run for mayor. If you want to run for Congress, run for Congress. You would probably make a good congressman. I think my son would make a better one, but if you want to get out and present yourself to the voters, you ought to do that. If your condition for running for either office has something to do with what I will or won't do, this is a wasteful conversation for both of us. I'm not going to agree to support you for a race that's three years down the road so you don't run against my son for a seat you claim you want to hold. I serve the people of the district, and if the people of the district want you in Congress, believe me, they'll vote for you. I'm going to support my son, and I think he's going to win. But whatever your decision is, I wish you the best. I hope it's a good race if you decide to run. If you don't run, I hope you support Harold Jr.

The entire meeting was about four minutes long. In the end, the commissioner didn't run.

Shortly after that meeting with the county commissioner, I officially announced for Congress. And my dad gave me his blessing—and simultaneously a test—in an important setting the following Saturday. He offered me the opportunity to speak at his annual congressional prayer breakfast, a spring ritual. It was my first formal speech as a candidate for Congress, and it was at my dad's most important political event.

I was nervous the morning of the speech. My friends Ed Stanton III and Robert White helped write the speech. The MC for the breakfast was my family's longtime friend Reverend Bill Adkins. He introduced me, hugged me, and whispered in my ear as I took to the podium, "Just relax; you're going to do fine."

This was actually the first time my dad was hearing me speak before a large audience since I had started exploring the race. There were 3,000 people at the breakfast. Everyone knew I would be speaking. My dad's supporters and opponents—Democrats and Republicans—all attended this breakfast, including the two men who ultimately entered the congressional race, State Representative Rufus Jones and State Senator Steve Cohen. Indeed, it was a big moment.

My speech went over well. When I finished, my father took the podium. "I want you all to know," he said, "that I was always going to support my son, but after hearing him speak this morning, I'm going to go out and work for him. And I'm going to ask everyone else here to work for him as well."

My dad's remarks marked an emotional turning point for me. His public show of support comforted, encouraged, and emboldened me. After the prayer breakfast speech, I returned to Ann Arbor to finish up the semester and graduate. But as encouraged as I was, there remained many political leaders in Memphis who were unconvinced that I could win. They didn't think I would be able to pull off a victory. I returned to Memphis the evening of May 11.

AT THIS POINT in the campaign, we didn't have much money. And without Ms. Jackson securing the kindergarten speeches, I wouldn't have had any places to go. The state president of the teachers' union and longtime family friend Velma Lois Jones advised me not to be dissuaded by my detractors—to keep my head and chin up and not stop working. I followed her advice. But because I had so little money, we could only afford to buy bumper stickers. We bought 25,000. My father believed that bumper stickers, when properly applied—no wrinkles, perfectly horizontal, centered when possible—could have a strong early effect in a campaign. They would transmit an impression of competence and dynamism. My dad believed that if we got these bumper stickers on 25,000 cars in a short period of time, it would energize all aspects of the campaign, including fund-raising. Fund-raising had been slow.

So, at headquarters, my father began holding classes on how to put bumper stickers on cars correctly—Bumper Sticker Training School, he called it. We had a lot of young volunteers working with us, and my dad was going to be absolutely sure that none of them got careless with bumper sticker application. He would summon them all up to the second floor for lessons. It was a mission for him.

Most people were delighted and honored to meet my dad, but they were meeting him in the slightly comical context of a tutorial on bumper sticker application. And he was serious. Although gracious and appreciative with the volunteers, he wasn't interested in sitting around and talking. He wanted people to learn and then get to the streets to put stickers on cars. He'd say, "Here are twenty-five bumper stickers. Now, give me your word that you're going to put them on properly, that you're going to put each one on a different car, and that you're going to do it in an hour—or less," he would say. He was the general.

He generated great enthusiasm. "Yes, sir!" the younger volunteers would say. Most finished in less than an hour. His biggest concern was that the bumper stickers be put on correctly—back window, lower left-hand corner, and straight. "A crooked bumper sticker is the sign of an unorganized campaign," my dad would say.

We fanned out across the city, putting bumper stickers on cars. Shopping centers, grocery stores, and outlet malls were target-rich environments. None of these places required invitations to gain admission. All it took was the courage to extend a hand and ask for support.

Before our first big bumper sticker purchase, my opponents began referring to me on the stump and in ads as "Junior," in an effort to belittle me. I had never been called "Junior" before. My family had always called me "Harold." My mother never called my dad "Harold" in the house. During Sunday dinners at my grandmother's home, with all my extended family around, everyone referred to me as "Baby Harold." "Junior" was never in the lexicon. My opponents used it so much, however, that everyone—supporters included—started referring to me as "Junior."

I'll never forget my dad explaining to me that I need not worry about being called Junior.

Don't get upset about it. You know what your opponents are trying to say, but think about this: When voters call you "Junior," they don't necessarily mean any harm by it. They may be innocently assuming that's what you've always been called. This can be a good thing. Let's not run from it—let's organize a campaign around it. It will do two things at once: remind my supporters that you're my son and that you may be inclined to do things the way I do them, and at the same time help establish your own political identity.

He was right. So all of our bumper stickers—all our campaign materials, in fact—said "Junior." When Steve Cohen and Rufus Jones called me Junior, they intended to convey something different than I was in my campaign materials. "What man means for ugly, God means for good," my mother said to me about using Junior.

I WAS EVERYWHERE. On the job every morning at 6:00 A.M. I would catch people early at breakfast places or intersections during the morning rush hour, go to events or visit schools or businesses during the day, work shopping center parking lots and intersections during the evening rush hour, and then try to make an evening event like a business or church dinner. If I had nothing scheduled in the evening, I would go to a popular dinner place and shake hands there.

Not having a well-financed campaign in the early stages was really a blessing in disguise. When you don't have a lot of money, you spend a lot of time listening to people. You listen more than you talk. I learned and learned as I listened.

And my opponents continued attacking me publicly. The attacks kept me in the press, and they were repetitive and un-original. "He's inexperienced, ignorant, arrogant, presumptu-ous," and so on. As we got deeper into summer, the media wanted to get a better feel for my candidacy. So I would invite them to meet me wherever I was going.

Reporters would watch me for a while and then interview the people who had talked to me. The responses surprised the press at first. People seemed to like me. Voters appreciated how hard I was working. Voters didn't think I was too young to be running for Congress, and many already had my bumper sticker on their cars.

Along with voters' responses to my kindergarten speeches, all of this new media attention was bolstering the cam-paign. We were underdogs, and we behaved like it. I compen-sated for a lack of money with energy, enthusiasm, and an understanding of the issues confronting voters. I looked like I was about ten years old, so many mothers and grand-mothers would talk about me as if I were a son or grandson. Increasingly, voters resented my opponents' personal attacks on me.

My response to the attacks was straightforward: "I wish my opponents would focus more on the unacceptably high drop-out rates in high schools across the district, the need for more summer jobs for our students, the need for more neighbor-hood health clinics, and the need to do more for seniors." My message was always positive. My campaign pollster, John Bakke, recommended that I stay positive but show more fight when it came to explaining how I would stand up for the district in Washington. In short, I had to demonstrate that I would fight like my dad fought.

The press even went to interview my dad about my progress as a candidate. He always said, "If you like me, you're going to love him." The interviewer said, "Why is that?" My dad said, "He's younger, he has more energy, he's better educated than I ever was, and I'm teaching him everything I know. And he's out there working his tail off every day to make this happen."

MY OPPONENTS GOT more aggressive—especially Steve Cohen. Polls showed Steve and me pulling away from Rufus Jones. Steve was turning his sights on me with increasing frequency. He raised the issue of corruption and nepotism in the Ford family and spoke of a Ford "dynasty," a tactic he thought would win him support from Republicans. Steve was openly urging Republicans to vote in the Democratic primary. "If you want to stop the Fords," he would say, "vote for me in the Democratic primary." Steve and his pollster, Jeff Pollock, had polls showing them winning the primary, but not without substantial Republican support. It was a clever strategy. So in response to this, I started calling Steve the "Great Republican Hope" in the Democratic primary. Steve and Jeff decided to accuse me of playing the race card, which was an explosive accusation. My co–campaign manager, Sharon Schieffer, was furious—and so was I. Steve wanted so badly to introduce race and was willing to distort my words to make race an issue.

But it didn't stop here. Steve—with help from Herenton—attacked me and lied about me throughout the primary. My age and inexperience were among the things he focused on. And my answer was the same every time.

"Whether you're twenty-six, thirty-six, or forty-six, whoever wins this race is going to be a freshman in Congress. You don't get extra points in Congress because you're older. My father was young when he was elected, and I think most people would agree that he's been an effective congressman."

Steve's attacks never matured. Neither Steve, Herenton, nor Rufus wanted to engage on the issues. They were more interested in attack politics. Ultimately, it was my work ethic and command of the issues that distinguished my candidacy from Steve's and Rufus's. The early hard work—the flights to and from Detroit and Memphis, the sixteen-hour days, and bumper stickering—was giving us our edge.

While on the trail talking to people, I was taking notes, so I knew very concretely what was going on in every part of the district. In my stump speeches, I referenced what I was learning from real people. I'd say, "I know my opponents have been busy, but they've been busy attacking me. They should probably be more focused on you. Instead of attacking me, they should be debating me on how we're going to make your life better."

I was challenging Steve and Rufus to be positive. Neither would do it.

◆   ◆

EVERYTHING CAME TO a head in the final Democratic primary debate. I'll never forget it. This was an important moment, because more and more voters were paying attention to what we were saying and how we were saying it. The primary was less than three weeks away. For the first time, the format would allow us to ask one another questions; voters still hadn't seen any face-to-face engagement. The first two debates had essentially been candidate forums. Direct exchanges were not allowed. The race was basically between Steve and me at this point.

Bakke believed that the only remaining reservation people had about me was whether I could hold my own in an adversarial setting. Going in, the press had covered many of the attacks against me, particularly from the Cohen camp, and some of the attacks had crossed the line. But he was undeterred. Again, his strategy was to win enough Republican support to win the Democratic primary. People wanted to see me respond to him directly. I had always taken the high road, but I would have to change course a little bit during the debate and be more aggressive. Voters wondered whether I could stand up to my critics, as my father had stood up to his for so many years while protecting the interests of the district. I had to project strength, humility, compassion, and courage. And strike the balance while doing so. I couldn't overreact and appear impulsive. I had to be a congressman.

My father chose not to attend the debate. I didn't understand his absence at first. At the end of the debate, I did. He knew that if he were in attendance, the cameras would find him—both during the debate and afterward. The night had to be about me. If I won, it had to be my victory.

The debate took place in the studio of the CBS affiliate, before a very small audience—twenty or thirty people at most. I prayed before the debate. I was thinking, "I've been wanting to do this all my life. This is what it's going to come down to." I was convinced the race would remain tight even if I did well, but if I flopped, it would give momentum to Steve—maybe enough momentum to win.

On the stage, I was seated directly across from Steve. Each candidate would be permitted to ask a question of whomever he wanted, with time allotted for rebuttals. The first part of the debate covered education, entitlements, and some local issues, but there was no meaningful debate. During the candidate Q&A session, I wanted to elevate the debate by injecting more substance and really challenging Steve and Rufus. Challenging Rufus was the equivalent of taking on Herenton. About thirty minutes into the debate, we were asked, "What has most disappointed you in this campaign?" I said I wished there had been more serious discussion about issues. I touched on national security, the budget, and energy policy. I stressed how many important issues there were and said that we could probably spend the entire debate on each one.

Then my big openings came. The first was when I had a chance to correct Steve on his falsely accusing me of saying that he was the "Great White Hope."

Steve indicated that I used the phrase "Great White Hope." That's not true. I've never used that phrase. I've never injected race into this campaign, and I won't do it going forward—nor will I engage in racial politics if I'm elected to Congress. Steve, I said you were the "Great Republican Hope" because, as you recall, you were quoted on the front page of the Memphis *Commercial Appeal* urging Republicans to vote in the Democratic primary. So let me be clear. You have injected race—I haven't. Let me also make clear to Democrats that you want Republicans to vote in our primary and pick our candidate for us. I believe that's wrong.

The second opportunity came late in the debate, when Steve asked me a direct question. I thought he might try to embarrass me by showing my lack of understanding of an important services program for Memphis. I was wrong. He tried a different approach. "Name three acts of personal courage that you have demonstrated in your life," he asked.

Steve was still refusing to take me seriously. He's not a bad guy but he thinks very highly of himself—sometimes too high. He honestly believed that he was the smartest and most courageous politician in Memphis and Nashville and now he deserved to go to Washington. He couldn't fathom or understand how anyone could question him on that. So, I responded,

Number one, I am running for Congress. It is an act of courage to enter public service, as anybody who has watched this race and listened to the things you've said about me and my family would know. You have to have courage to expose yourself to attacks. Two, when my dad was tried for something he didn't do, the way he conducted himself was an act of great courage. I drew inspiration from him—from the strength and resiliency he embodied during an incredibly painful time. Three, and I can't call this an act of courage on my part, but as I've had a chance to travel around this district and listen to people talk about their dreams and aspirations, I've drawn courage from them. I've spoken at kindergarten graduations and listened to five- and six-year-olds and to so many other students at school events across the city. I've talked to people at cookouts and church meetings, at barber-shops and beauty shops. And if given a chance to go to Congress, I promise that I will show courage when I stand up for the people of this district—and I don't just intend to fight for what they believe in, I intend to achieve the results they deserve.

In a debate, never ask a question if you don't know the answer. Steve just stared at me incredulously. The moment he had depended on so heavily to disqualify me had not materialized. Again, Dr. Taft-Morales and Mr. Wilmore would have been proud.

My answer on courage dominated media coverage of the debate. Steve did not come off well. I had carefully and successfully walked the fine line of standing up for myself while maintaining composure and showing that I had more than enough fight to stand up for the people of the district. My father was in Washington, and he called John Bakke and me right after the debate. "How do you think he did?" he asked John.

"He won the debate and the race tonight," John said.

"What do you mean he won the race?" my dad asked.

"He won," he said. "His answer on courage—that answer is going to get a lot of media attention. That answer is going to be talked about. He didn't hesitate. He looked like a congressman. That's exactly what undecided voters needed to see."

He was right. I went on to win the Democratic primary over Steve Cohen by twenty points. I faced a spirited fight in the general election from my Republican opponent, Rod De-Berry. Rod was a young African American corporate executive at a big Memphis company. He had run unsuccessfully against my dad two years earlier. He was a formidable opponent who was helped by the fact that the Republican National Convention (RNC) spent huge dollars in Tennessee on behalf of the Dole-Kemp 1996 presidential ticket. In turn, I had to keep borrowing and spending money to make sure that I got Democrats out to the polls. In the end, I won by twenty points—and I was $1 million in debt.

On the night of my victory, my dad took me aside and told me something I've never forgotten. He said, "Two things you need to remember when you go to Washington. One, always take care of the people. And two, always take care of the people." I was still learning.

TERMS *of* SERVICE

L IVING UP TO THE CONSTITUENT-SERVICE STAN-
dards my dad set was my chief challenge and priority
when I got to Congress, but such was my dad's relationship with his constituents that they continued to contact
him for months after I took office. He would relay the messages to me, and I remember finally asking him, "Why don't
they just call me in the office to ask for help?"

"You should probably figure that out sooner rather than
later," he responded with his characteristic directness. "In the
meantime, why don't you call the person back and get to work
on the problem?" And I did and would.

Soon after I got to Congress, the Memphis *Commercial Appeal* did a story on my constituent-service efforts. The reporter
interviewed one of my senior staffers, Scott Keefer, who had
also worked for my father. What was the biggest difference, he
asked Scott, between working for me and working for my father? Scott emphasized that my father and I shared the same
work ethic and commitment to our constituents, but added,
quite innocently, "I got spoiled working for his father, because

government agencies responded more quickly to constituent inquiry. With his dad, I'd call an agency at 9:30 A.M. and get a response, if not a resolution, by noon. With the new congressman, it can take an entire day."

The reporter asked, "You mean Harold Jr.'s slower and less effective?"

"No, he's effective," Scott replied, "but his dad had twenty-two years of experience, belonged to the majority party, and served on the Ways and Means Committee. Harold Jr. will figure it out and be fine. Watch and see."

THE MORNING AFTER my victory in Tennessee, I started preparing my constituent-service operation. I held my first transition meeting in my dad's Memphis office, which I later took over. On that first morning, I was handed his constituent casebooks. From then until I left for Washington, I went into his office every day to study cases. The more time I spent doing it, the more I realized how much more there was to learn about casework. Each case had its own context, its own complexities, its own texture.

My dad's advice was threefold. First, respond to every call and letter. He told me that people would contact me because they were unable to get a response from anyone else. A return call was an important part of the journey. Second, establish a system to track cases from initial request to final resolution. That would allow me to assess the quality of my staff's work and identify and replicate the most efficient system to resolve cases. Third, personally handle three or four cases every few weeks. It was crucial, he said, to remain in direct touch with constituents and stay alert to any new bureaucratic obstacles at federal and state agencies or staff issues that crop up.

I set to work implementing this system right away. I held on to several of my dad's caseworkers. When I hired new people, the only requirement was that they be willing to do casework—*no one was above doing the most important work in the office.*

There was no way to learn casework other than to put in the time it took to understand people's problems and master resolving them. I worked my tail off to put the best case resolution system in place that I could. It quickly became apparent that getting casework resolution right was the most important thing I could do to ensure a successful first term—and to get reelected to a second term. The enormous loyalty my dad enjoyed from constituents was predominantly due to what he told me the night I won: "Always take care of your constituents." During my first two years in office, I responded with a handwritten note to every piece of mail addressed to me. If you sent me a letter and had a problem with an employer or a Social Security benefit or a Medicare payment, I would write back to say, "I am looking into it and thanks for contacting your congressional office."

One of the main tasks of my deputy chief of staff was to provide regular summaries of every piece of constituent mail the office received. The summaries included contact information, a summary of the letter, the name of the staffer assigned to the case, and a note on any progress made to date. After a day of committee meetings and votes on the House floor, I would return to the office and examine every piece of mail and every phone request that had come in. When I arrived in Memphis on the weekends, I received similar summaries from my Memphis office director. After reviewing it all, I would ask my staffers about it: Did you get this or that letter? Where are you on it? Whatever the case, I wanted to know what progress was being made.

During my first year in Congress, I rarely left my Washington office before 11:00 P.M. For the first nine months, I lived with my mother in the home I grew up in because I owed so much money after my campaign that I couldn't afford an apartment. It hardly registered that I was staying with my mom because of the long hours I kept. I'd leave the office, get to my mom's house twenty minutes later, sink into the couch, turn on the TV, fall asleep, get up at 6:00 A.M. to work out, and arrive at the office at 7:30 A.M.

I wrote between fifty and seventy-five notes to my constituents every day—or about 1,500 handwritten notes a month. I always wanted to maintain personal contact with my constituents—my "bosses," as I called people in Memphis. I believed that a note from me acknowledging a request, commending an achievement, or championing a worthy endeavor would deepen my connection to my constituents. I praised the academic and athletic accomplishments of students and teachers, congratulated small-business owners and entrepreneurs for passing commercial milestones, and recognized law enforcement, community leaders, and teachers for initiatives that improved the quality of life in the district. When I went home and traveled around Memphis, it was deeply gratifying to see my notes framed and hung on the walls in doctors' offices, school classrooms, corporate headquarters, social service agencies, and individual homes.

I almost always took casework materials with me on my flights to and from Memphis. I remember spending the duration of one flight intently writing notes to constituents and tracking cases using phone message sheets and mail summaries. A Memphis businessman was sitting next to me on one flight from D.C. to Memphis during the late spring of 1997. He was cordial but not particularly friendly. We chatted briefly after sitting down, and then I took out my casework to start writing notes and tracking casework resolution. The businessman fell asleep. About halfway through the flight, he awakened, watched me work for a while, and said, "Hey, Congressman, do you ever stop working?"

I smiled and said, jokingly, "I'll take a break after you vote for me a few times."

Laughing, he replied, "You didn't get my vote the first time, but after seeing how hard you're working, you'll get it the next time. And I'm going to tell everyone I know who didn't vote for you—which is quite a few people—that you're the hardest-working politician I've ever seen."

My goal was to write 40,000 handwritten notes to constituents during my first two years in office. I thought that if I combined that kind of outreach with visits to places like health clinics, schools, beauty salons, barbershops, churches, senior centers, restaurants, recreation centers, and public libraries, I would gain a much better understanding of the needs of my constituents; they would gain a much better understanding of me; and I would be able to represent them better and more fully.

I spent countless hours crisscrossing the district and attending events. I continually spoke at elementary, middle, and high schools. I made a point of visiting every public school in the district during the first two years. I wanted continued first-hand knowledge of the challenges facing the students, the teachers, and the school system as a whole. These visits and interactions proved invaluable for my service on the House Education and Workforce Committee.

My constituents expected this kind of work ethic. It built trust between them and me. As my first term progressed and I continued to travel the district and improve my constituent-service operation, the trust was growing. I was getting lots of practice.

THE REQUESTS AND cases themselves were voluminous and diverse. There were lots of solicitations for donations to community events. Nonprofits of all stripes sought financial support. I often made contributions to proven organizations through my campaign funds. Consistent with my dad's time in office, the bill disputes with Memphis Light, Gas and Water remained a prominent part of our work. People had disagreements with their banks. Many people sought counseling on how to buy a home or wanted advice on altering or just keeping up with their mortgage payments. There were landlord-tenant issues. Schools and hospitals and health clinics wanted to know how they could secure federal grants or otherwise access federal money.

The congressional office often helped guide people through disparate mazes of state and federal bureaucracies. A huge number of cases involved veterans, immigration, and disability claims. As a result, I had staffers who became experts in certain case areas.

One case in particular brought me back to my earliest experiences with constituent service and served as a visceral reminder of the necessity and urgency of casework. If the phone rang more than four times, I would answer it. I had a receptionist, but I also had a rule in the office: No one was above answering constituent calls. One day, I took a complaint from a woman whose property management company was refusing to make an essential repair. Sounded familiar. She had been waiting for more than three weeks. I called the property management company to ask about it. I told them who I was and what I was calling about, and I said I was having trouble understanding why it was taking them so long to solve the problem. They told me they would resolve it that day. They were somewhat embarrassed that I had called them. I relayed the good news to my constituent and told her to phone me back if there was a problem.

To my surprise, she called back late the next day and told me that the property management company had neither fixed the problem nor called her back about it. I was pissed that I had been lied to. I called the property management company office and said to the manager, "Y'all explained to me yesterday that you were going to get something done. I just spoke with your tenant, and learned that you didn't do what you said you would. I wish you would just have told me you couldn't do it. If I told you I was going to do something, I'd do it, and I'd do it when I told you I was going to do it."

The woman who answered the phone said, "I'm sorry. I'm going to pull the file up right now. Can you hold for one second, Congressman?"

She thought she'd pushed the hold button, but she hadn't. Someone in the room there said, "I can't believe this motherf— called us back. Can you believe this sh—? Can you believe that bit— called him again?"

I listened for a moment longer and then said, "When you guys finish talking about your tenant and me, do you think you could get around to fixing the problem in her place?"

There was silence on the other end of the phone.

The woman got her apartment repaired that night, and I filed a complaint about the property management company. I don't recall ever getting a complaint about that property management company again.

My dad and family taught me about the importance of giving. The message was driven home during the holidays with my father's "Operation Happy Christmas" giveaway to families in need. It was a simple nonprofit—no overhead, no staff, no office space—designed to rally the Memphis business community behind an effort to provide roughly $50 worth of groceries to hardworking families just barely making it.

My dad started the giveaway shortly after he was elected to the Tennessee legislature in 1970. He gave away bikes for

Christmas from the family funeral home in South Memphis. It evolved and grew with the help of corporate and nonprofit partners into an effort and event that always happened the Saturday before Christmas that resulted in more than five thousand $50 boxes of groceries being given out to families across the Memphis area. I continued the tradition while in Congress, with the volunteer help of my staffers including Sherman Greer, Clay Perry, and John Freeman, and even today—while living in New York—I continue the tradition in Memphis.

IMPROVING MY CONSTITUENT-SERVICE work enabled me to be more aggressive with my legislative work. When you are responsive to your district, as my dad explained, you can be a better, more daring, and more effective policymaker. I knew that if voters trusted and believed in me as a problem solver at home, they would trust me to solve problems in Washington. And if my ideas challenged conventional liberal ideology, voters were more willing to give me the benefit of the doubt if they trusted me. Furthermore, the better I understood the needs and hopes of my constituents—presumably—the more effective I could be as a legislator. In short, I was more equipped to propose and support legislation that could improve the lives of people.

I wanted to introduce legislation to reform education and housing policy, simplify the tax code, and change the way credit bureaus calculated and made available credit scores. My reform approach wasn't easy to categorize politically. I approached policy formation literally, believing that including the best ideas, regardless of their political origins, usually guaranteed the best policy outcome. I wasn't afraid to work with Republicans to achieve the best legislative end.

One Saturday afternoon, early in my first term, I was in my district congressional office studying various state legislation on credit scores. I was preparing to propose federal legislation mandating transparency around consumer credit scores. I took a break to read the business section of the Memphis *Commercial Appeal* and came across an article about Arnold Perl, the chairman of the local airport authority. I had met Arnold at the county mayor's Christmas party several months earlier. In the article, Arnold was making a strong case for a third runway—a "world runway," as he called it—at Memphis International Airport. Memphis needed $75 million to complete the project. The "world runway" would allow FedEx, Memphis's largest employer, to fly planes directly from Memphis to important destinations in Asia, whose markets were growing rapidly, and FedEx's continued penetration would expand job opportunities in Memphis.

I was intrigued. I put down the paper and phoned Jay Lindy, my closest confidant in the district after my father, and then Doyle Cloud, a senior government affairs officer for FedEx.

I asked Jay to tell me more about Arnold, and I asked Doyle how important the runway was to Fred Smith, FedEx's chairman and CEO. Jay told me that Arnold was smart, respected, capable, and disarmingly hard-charging. Doyle told me that

FedEx absolutely needed the runway if it was to continue growing in Memphis.

Jay got me Arnold's number and I phoned him. We hit it off instantly. He shared with me his Republican leanings but assured me that his only political interest in the runway was "winning for Memphis." We had a common interest. I was able to arrange a meeting with Arnold, the president of the airport authority, Larry Cox, and another board member, Tommy Farnsworth, at the office of the U.S. secretary of transportation, Rodney Slater—an old friend—the following week. Arnold was surprised that I moved so quickly to get a meeting with the secretary.

Secretary Slater was aware that the Memphis airport needed funding, but at the time, money was tight for airport expansion projects. To win federal dollars, Memphis would have to demonstrate that the nation as a whole would benefit from a $75 million investment in the Memphis airport.

For my district, the stakes were high. We went to work on it. The runway project would create new jobs, and it could potentially attract manufacturing and high-tech firms, among other companies, to the Memphis area. Companies might consider headquartering in Memphis. Other companies might consider relocating there.

We had a strong argument. By metric tonnage, Memphis International Airport was the largest cargo airport in the world. FedEx is an important global company and franchise. The Memphis region's economic stability and growth depended on it, and expanding capacity would create economic opportunities for companies all over the country and the world. Furthermore, the airport's passenger traffic was among the fastest growing in the nation, largely due to Northwest Airlines' hub there. Finally, Memphis International was among the most critical elements of the country's air-traffic-management system.

Slater was impressed with Arnold's presentation. He was good. After the meeting, Slater confided to me that the project was doable but more work needed to be done. There were many other airports, he said, seeking expansion funds. In political speak, I interpreted that to mean: You need to marshal as much support as possible from your colleagues and the White House.

I immediately went to work—and so did Arnold. I stroked the fragile egos of my colleagues on the powerful House Appropriations Committee. I lobbied congressmen whose districts depended on Memphis International for commercial and passenger service. I began making the argument for runway expansion to the Clinton White House, knowing that Vice President Al Gore would be most influential.

Fortunately, I was close to Gene Sperling, one of President Clinton's chief economic advisers. I reminded him of the importance of the expansion project every chance I got. My former boss on the Clinton transition team, Thurgood "Goody" Marshall, Jr., was a senior aide to Vice President Gore. I'm sure Goody grew sick of my calls, but that's what I wanted. I wanted him and everyone else in the White House to get so sick of my persistence that they would agree to release the money quickly.

My colleague and friend Marion Berry, whose Arkansas district was connected to mine by the I-40 bridge spanning the Mississippi River, was instrumental in winning support for the project. He leaned on his Arkansas colleagues in Congress and weighed in with the White House. A farmer and a former businessman, Marion had known President Clinton for many years and had worked in the White House as his special adviser on agriculture and rural economic development before his election to Congress in 1996. I didn't have a better friend in Congress than Marion.

I worked my fellow Tennessee congressmen John Tanner and Ed Bryant, whose congressional districts abutted mine and stood to benefit greatly from the project. Conveniently, we often flew home together after votes on Thursdays, so I lobbied them then.

What better way to demonstrate the Memphis airport's importance to their districts, I thought, than by explaining it to them while they were flying into Memphis in order to get home for the weekend.

And because Northwest Airlines has its hub in Memphis, many of my colleagues from Louisiana, Mississippi, Kansas, and Oklahoma often connected in Memphis. Whenever I ran into them, I pulled them aside and lobbied them, too.

Arnold didn't let up, either. He and his team were in Washington at least once a month lobbying for the project. He was terrific. Arnold became my ambassador to the business community in Memphis. He made it a point to tell his Republican clients and friends how helpful I was and how easy I was to work with.

Our efforts started yielding fruit. We received a $9 million Department of Transportation grant in March of 1997 and an additional $5 million in September for airport improvement, including construction associated with the proposed new runway. But we still lacked the remaining $61 million.

Shortly after the $5 million installment, Congress was preparing to vote on "fast-track" trade legislation. President Clinton wanted the control to negotiate trade agreements on the nation's behalf, which I supported.

Many Democrats influenced by labor were opposed to fast track. Labor wanted tougher environmental and workplace standards in any trade agreement. An absence of strict rules, they argued, would translate into low wages abroad and a loss of American jobs. I didn't disagree with them but I believed Clinton could be trusted to negotiate tough standards and that the United States should never be afraid of competition from anywhere. Clinton argued that U.S. ingenuity and entrepreneurship would make us strong in the face of any global competition. These agreements would ensure U.S. access to foreign markets.

I supported the president and agreed that the United States should never shy away from competition. Moreover, increased trade with developing nations would raise living standards in those nations, which, I believed, would make those nations more reliable global partners in every way. And there was one more reason for supporting fast track, as I told the president during a meeting at the White House. His name was Al Gore. I was for Gore 2000 even in 1997. If Gore thought it was good for the working man, that was added reason to vote for it. In the end, the White House failed to persuade enough Democrats to support fast track. Clinton had secured more than 175 Republican votes, but the Republicans didn't want to deliver such a big victory to a Democratic president if two-thirds of the Democratic caucus was going to oppose their president. When it became clear that no more than forty House Democrats would vote with Clinton, fast track was dead. In the end, the president had been rebuked by his own party.

On the night the legislation died, I was working late in my D.C. office. My legislative director knocked on my door to tell me that the president was on the phone. President Clinton graciously thanked me for my support and expressed his hope that we would get another chance to pass fast-track legislation. I told the president I thought it was unfortunate that our party would do this to him but that I would be there for him if he wanted to do it again. The conversation lasted two or three minutes. Thirty seconds after I hung up with Clinton, the same staffer came running back in to tell me that the White House was on the phone again. It was Gene Sperling this time. "Hey, we gave it a great try," Sperling said, "and I just wanted to thank you myself." I repeated what I had said to Clinton, and added, "The Republicans would never have done this to a Republican president. It's asinine that we couldn't come up with fifty to sixty votes, and it explains why we Democrats lose more than we win at the national level."

"The sad thing," Sperling said, "is that the U.S. worker is going to get doubly screwed without a trade agreement. Not only will U.S. companies be treated unfairly in foreign markets and have difficulty selling U.S. products, but the Chinese will seize the opportunity to gain market share and take more U.S. jobs."

He was right.

What he said next, however, would make my first term in Congress legislatively meaningful for my district.

"You were the only congressman who pledged support for the president without asking for something," Sperling said, meaning that I hadn't demanded a bridge or a new highway in my district in exchange for my vote. "The president and vice president are very appreciative."

I said, "Hey, thank you, but understand that I didn't pledge my support for any reason other than I believed the vote I was about to cast was the right one. But if y'all are handing out goodies, we sure do need some help building this big runway in Memphis."

"Have a good night, Congressman," Gene responded.

A few weeks later, I received a routine call from Vice President Al Gore. But the purpose of this call was bigger than usual—he informed me that the Memphis International Airport would receive more than $60 million in infrastructure improvement funding in the coming days. I thanked him and said I looked forward to joining him in Memphis to announce the grant.

I had helped deliver a $75 million grant as a freshman congressman in the minority party. "No one deserves more credit than Harold Ford, Jr., for making this happen," Marion Berry said at the announcement. It was big.

◆   ◆

THROUGHOUT MY TENURE in Congress, talk abounded about how far my views diverged from my father's. I was perceived as being to his right. Not long after I was elected, Dana Milbank did a story on me for *The New York Times Magazine* called "Harold Ford Jr. Storms His Father's House."

Dana's a good guy. His story was fair, but I never thought consciously about breaking with my father's views, nor did I think my positions were incompatible with his. In fact, I viewed my positions as being encouraged and inspired by my father's.

But my alignment with the Blue Dogs (i.e., moderate Democrats) in Congress troubled some of my dad's former liberal colleagues. Early on, my colleagues were surprised by my unapologetic support for education reform and charter schools, my commitment to balanced budgets, and my frustration with my party's reflexive and puzzling opposition to cutting small-business taxes. Admittedly, it was a different approach from my father's. What some of my critics never accepted, and do not accept even to this day, is that my views were not the result of raw political ambition. Conversely, my views reflected an open-minded approach to achieving a set of outcomes— outcomes that mirrored those of liberals and progressives. My dad and I shared—and continue to share—a common vision for outcomes on education, housing, taxes, and fiscal policy. When my dad was asked about my voting record, he would often say, "You know, Harold's from a different era. A different time. He grew up in different circumstances and had different experiences than I did. If I'd grown up the way he did, I'd probably be casting the same votes he's casting."

To the surprise of some, my father never called before a big vote trying to sway me one way or the other. It was always me calling him, asking for advice. And his message was always the same: "You should worry about one thing: whether or not the voters in the district believe in, understand, and support what you're doing. As long as they do, you're fine."

I followed that path with zeal. But the criticism didn't abate. I was falsely accused of being a sellout by liberals. It didn't bother me. In fact, it emboldened me.

The policies I supported came right out of what I felt the people in my district needed and wanted. My constituents wanted accountability. They wanted better results. I supported charter schools because I believed new approaches were needed to teach kids who were trapped in failing schools. I voted to cut middle class taxes and expand the EITC because everyone deserved a tax break. I voted to allow mixed-income public housing projects because I thought income diversity would benefit everyone in public housing. Liberals in my district and in Congress who opposed me didn't appreciate, I believed, the change in approach. They wanted to continue using the same approaches. I didn't fear trying something different, even if it meant failing. If we failed, we'd try something else. Sometimes when speaking before liberal and skeptical audiences in Memphis and Washington about education reform, I would defend charter school and voucher efforts by saying, "If we pursue vigorous education reform for a year or two and it fails, we can always return the kids to the terrible education setting they were in before we tried to make it better. Then we should try again until we make it better for kids. We politicians are blessed these kids can't vote; if they could, they'd vote us all out of office because of the repeated lies we tell them about how we're going to improve their schools year after year. We should all be ashamed of ourselves for failing them." Each time I cast a vote, I did so with the interests of my constituents foremost in my mind.

"MOST PEOPLE WHO come to Washington," my father told me, "will just want to see you. If you put aside the special interest groups and the lobbyists, you'll find that people want nothing more than to talk to and spend time with their congressman. That's true even when constituents come up to lobby legislation."

During my five terms in Congress, if you were from Memphis and I was in town, I would meet with you personally. Even when I was in committee hearings or on the floor, I would have my staff bring constituents to me. There are rooms right off the House floor where congressmen meet with constituents. When the president or foreign dignitary speaks to a joint session of Congress, the First Lady or the dignitary's guests sit in the gallery. The gallery is usually reserved for constituent groups. You can take a group up there and let them sit and watch the proceedings. People love being in the Capitol, and I would often take my constituents into the gallery and get them seated. I spent nearly as much time doing that as anything else, and, frankly, I preferred it to sitting with lobbyists or national interest groups.

When we'd get visits from schools—elementary, middle, and high school—I would take the students into the gallery of the House and then out onto the Capitol steps. I called it the classroom on the steps. I wanted to give them a sense of where I worked and teach a lesson on how the different branches of government functioned.

I would quiz the kids about the functions of the three branches of government. Often, kids didn't raise their hands at first. Unfortunately, most were uncertain about the respective functions of the three branches. Some of the younger kids had no idea what I was talking about. But one might speak up and say, "Congress passes the laws," and we would build on that. After some discussion, I'd enforce the message: "Now assume that the House of Representatives passed a bill that mandated that sixth-graders"—or whatever grade they were in—"had to do three hours of homework each night, have at least two vegetables every night for dinner, and watch only one hour of TV a week. And that the bill prohibited soda or fast-food consumption except on Saturday afternoons and allowed movie-going only once a month."

I would tailor the legislation to the age group. For instance, if the group was high school seniors, the law would limit car privileges to one weekend a month and all social gatherings and movies to once every two months.

Continuing, I'd say, "So that's the new law, and anyone who broke it would be sentenced to a minors' jail for thirty days for every single violation." The kids would make noises and look at one another as if to say, "Is he crazy? Is he kidding?"

"Now, if the House passed it, what's the other side of the Capitol called?"

"The Senate," someone would yell.

"Assume the Senate passed it. Where would it go to be signed into law?"

"The president," someone would nervously exclaim.

"That's right," I'd say. "The president has to sign it for it to become an enforceable law."

Then I'd say, "The great thing about the system is if there are laws that we don't like, we can challenge them in the courts. Right across the way there is the Supreme Court, the highest court in the land. So give me a sense: Who would like to get rid of this bill I talked about?" More often than not, every hand would shoot up, followed by the outburst, "I would!" And I'd say, "So your parents, or maybe another group, like soda and Hollywood movie companies, would file a lawsuit on your behalf. These companies would want to protect you and their profits. The lawsuit for you would be filed in downtown Memphis, in the federal building where my office is, and where the courts are." I would continue building the drama, walking them through the trial and getting them all excited. The younger kids would always be looking at me with anticipation, hoping that the end of the story would reverse things in their favor. And then I'd say, "And more likely than not, they would *strike this law down*!" And all the kids would clap loudly.

"And if all of this doesn't work, you have another option. You could go to the polls—*you* can't, until you are eighteen—but you could tell your parents and your teachers and your pastor to go to the polls and vote against any politician who supported this bill. They could vote against *me* if I supported the bill. But something you need to be assured of—*I would never vote for that bill.*" And everyone would clap again.

They would laugh and say, "We knew *you* wouldn't!" But they would all invariably breathe a sigh of relief. I'd say, "But if I did vote for it, you could go to the polls or have your parents go to the polls and vote me out of office. The thing you guys need to understand is that in many countries around the world people don't have the rights and protection we have in this country. The majority of people in this world don't enjoy the checks and balances we take for granted. Our country is great for many reasons—none more important than the way our government is organized. And we owe that to our Constitution. When you get home, make it a point to pay closer attention when it comes time to study it." And if they were old enough, I'd urge them to read it again.

Spending time with these students was the right thing to do for many reasons. (Some of the press criticized me even for this—I couldn't escape their wrath.) Kids had launched my first campaign for Congress. Kindergartners and fifth- and sixth-graders had listened to me when no one else would—or cared to, for that matter. For me, taking kids around the Capitol complex was the equivalent of politicians thanking big donors by lavishing personal time and gratitude on them. It was important to me to enliven the experience of learning about government. I took it for granted that all kids were like me and had a deep interest in learning how government worked. That wasn't the case for many young people. I wanted to do my part to help kids understand and respect the process of governing.

I always ended my lesson on the steps by asking the kids to

raise their right hand and take a pledge: to work hard, play by the rules, and keep God first. It was the same pledge I had asked those kindergartners and fifth- and sixth-graders to take in the spring of 1996 at the end of my graduation speeches. In fact, it was the same—although unspoken—pledge my grandmother and mother had made me take as a kid. And kids can't be reminded enough how important work, discipline, and faith are. I was still learning.

CONSCIENTIOUS OBJECTIONS

D URING MY TIME IN CONGRESS, I WAS FORTUNATE to enjoy great popularity at home and strong relationships with most of my colleagues, especially those from Tennessee. However, I was often at odds with the House Democratic leadership. From the moment I arrived, unlike many of my Democratic colleagues, I refused to remain silent when I disagreed with the Democratic leadership on issues of import.

I'll never forget standing in Minority Leader Dick Gephardt's office as a twenty-six-year-old, newly elected freshman congressman, politely but firmly demanding that my freshman class be given seats on the House's three most influential committees: Ways and Means, Appropriations, and Commerce.

My class was big—there were 43 of us out of 206 in the Democratic caucus—but the Democratic leadership had informed us that assignments to the "exclusives," as the three committees are known, would not be available. Members of the leadership claimed that they couldn't offer any slots because the Republicans had reduced the ratios of Democrats to Republicans on the committees, and senior Democrats were already waiting for slots.

Some freshmen accepted that argument, but I didn't. It was unfair by the numbers, and I took issue with what I saw as the Democrats' strict adherence to the seniority rule. Many in the caucus had served for twenty or more years, and the attitude was "We reward seniority." Twenty years of public service is obviously worthy of respect, but seniority alone shouldn't determine everything, I thought.

Soon after arriving in Washington, I ran to be president of the freshman class, and I won partly by promising to work tirelessly and fearlessly to secure committee seats. I also owed my victory to a diverse coalition of supporters, including Silvestre Reyes, Rubén Hinojosa, and Max Sandlin from Texas and Marion Berry from Arkansas. I'll never forget Marion saying to me, "I'll make you a deal—I'll get all the rednecks to vote for you, you get some of the others, and we'll win this thing." Our class had decided to split the presidency among four people, and the four of us were responsible for conveying our concerns to the leadership. I dutifully expressed our concerns to the leadership about legislative priorities and committee seats. "There are forty-three of us," I wrote, "and at the very least, we deserve one freshman on each of these exclusive committees."

Gephardt's staff was dismissive—to characterize it generously. I believed that the leadership needed to change course. Democrats had kept the same basic leadership team in place after the loss of 1994. I argued that the current Democratic team had lost the majority in 1994, and that in the real world, running a company into the ground gets you fired. A publicly traded company's board of directors would have fired the Democratic leadership by now if it were a company—not to mention that a pro sports franchise would likely have fired the coach after a few losing seasons.

Gephardt's staff disliked me with a passion. Gephardt himself was always gracious. I actually liked and respected him—still do. The Democratic leaders did not appreciate this kind of resistance, and they hadn't seen it coming because they hadn't taken me seriously. Many had assumed I was going to lose my primary to Steve Cohen, and none of the Democratic leadership had supported me, except Bill Richardson. I will never forget a conversation I had with Steny Hoyer a year into my first term. We were in the Democratic cloakroom, off the House floor, and he said, "I have to tell you, when you were elected, I thought to myself, 'This guy is a lightweight who had his seat handed to him by his father.' But I've been pleasantly surprised, and I look forward to working with you." I liked and respected Steny greatly, and still do, but I couldn't resist jokingly saying, "Thanks, Steny. I thought the same thing about you when I got here, and you proved me wrong, too." I probably shouldn't have said it, but I couldn't resist.

"The people in my district didn't elect a twenty-six-year-old freshman. They elected a congressman. My job is to represent them in Washington, and if I don't do it effectively, they shouldn't reelect me." It was the answer I repeatedly gave to the Memphis press when I was asked if I thought a freshman could fully and effectively serve Memphis.

I wasn't overconfident when I got to Congress, but I wasn't nervous either. I understood that we were all equals, and I wasn't going to be pushed around. I always treated Democratic leaders with due deference and respected the formalities of the institution, but they knew where I stood. In fact, I often addressed my senior colleagues as "Mr." or "Mrs." because I had known so many of them from childhood. But I stood firm on policy.

JUNIOR CONGRESSPEOPLE IN either party generally sit in the back of the room during meetings—hence the name "backbenchers." In my class, we backbenchers would often sit in meetings and listen to the Democratic leadership develop policy and political responses to the Republican majority. We would think, "Why are we doing this? Why are we pursuing this particular strategy?" Regardless of the issue, the political strategy was so predictable—on tax cuts, fight the Republicans; on education reform, resist the Republicans; on defense spending, rebut the Republicans; on promoting small business, thwart the Republicans. We rarely offered anything new on any hard issue. The Republicans undoubtedly led the country down a destructive and dangerous path of fiscal and foreign policy, but my party countered with weak ideas for change. I was not alone in questioning the wisdom of the party leadership. Many of us realized that the Democrats lacked a coherent strategy to win elections in 1998, 2000, and 2002.

From 1997 to 2001, the House Democratic leadership and caucus reinforced the worst impressions the American people had of national Democrats. Although a Democrat had been reelected to the White House for the first time since FDR, the national message espoused by Clinton didn't always comport with the national message of House Democrats—House Democrats were seen as out of the mainstream fiscally and socially.

The nation seemed to define and even to appreciate the House Democrats' role as the check against Republican excesses in Congress—and ultimately the presidential veto as the final stopper if the House Democrats couldn't do it. Many of my Democratic colleagues didn't understand this phenomenon. They would get so excited by generic polls in the early spring of an election year showing that voters preferred Democrats in Congress to govern on education and health care by wide margins. The same polls would show Republicans with similarly wide margins on national security and defense issues, especially after 2001. Some polls would even show a majority of voters nationally preferring a Democratic majority over a Republican one. These polls inspired and emboldened the Democratic leadership. The only problem was that these springtime polls never translated into fall victories.

After Republicans retained their majorities in 1998 and 2000—albeit smaller majorities—my frustration grew, because we were employing the same approaches wrapped around the same tired slogans of "win back the majority" or "take back the majority."

It was hard for me to understand House Democrats' fidelity to these slogans, because by 2001, the majority of House Democrats had never served in the majority. In short, it had never been ours to lose. And most Americans didn't think of

Democrats as needing to win back anything. The American people weren't fixated on the Republican takeover of 1994. They were thinking about their own challenges—rising gas prices, high taxes, and exploding health and child care costs. And they were worried about their future.

The Republicans stuck to their formula—accusing Democrats of wanting higher taxes and bigger government while being weak on security. Voters clearly didn't trust us enough on those issues, and Republicans were much better at communicating their message. A majority of Americans accepted the Republican governing frame of a smaller government and a tougher foreign policy. In fact, in 2000, Bush ran for president on the foreign policy plank of no more foreign nation-building. Bush accused Clinton and Democrats of draining precious U.S. tax dollars on nation-building instead of investing in and defending vital U.S. national interests abroad. And now Bush was about to embark on the most ambitious nation-building exercise in a generation.

From 1992 to 2000, Bill Clinton, Al Gore, and the congressional Democrats helped lead America to record economic expansion and college matriculation rates, 22 million new jobs, a balanced budget, historic welfare reform, and budget surpluses in the final years of Clinton's second term. But in the 2000 election, House Democrats couldn't win a majority, and my dear friend, Vice President Al Gore, couldn't win either.

Our national message hadn't connected. And House Democrats had misread the electorate . . . again.

◆　　　◆

2000 WAS A big year for me politically for another reason. I was given the chance by Vice President Gore to deliver the keynote address at the Democratic National Convention (DNC) in Los Angeles. It was an enormous honor for anyone, especially a thirty-year-old, two-term congressman. The preparation for and lead-up to the speech was one of the more instructive political lessons I had.

I phoned my dad to tell him the news right after I learned I'd be the speaker and to consult with him on how to handle the media. His advice: "Call the editor of the *Commercial Appeal* and give him a blow-by-blow of what happened to earn this honor and then preview your speech for him." This was against my intuition because I thought the *Commercial Appeal*'s coverage of me was shallow, mean-spirited, and unfair. "Why give it to them?" I asked my dad scornfully.

"Because most of the national press has no clue who you are, and most of the national press corps will be lazy in trying to learn about you and your politics," my dad answered swiftly. "They [the national press] will look to your local newspaper first, and maybe only, to learn about you, your politics, and the developments leading up to your getting the nod from Al to give the speech," he finished.

He was right. The *Commercial Appeal* was appreciative to get the first sit-down with me and consequently wrote an honest and positive piece that served as the basis for all the national pieces that were done leading up to the speech.

The 2000 DNC convention was in Los Angeles. I arrived in LA the weekend before the convention and started to write and prepare for the speech. One of my best friends, Chad

Brownstein, picked me up from the airport. In LA I was meeting another dear friend and law school classmate, Jason Levien, who was going to help me with the speech. Editorial control for the speech's content was to be shared between me and Vice President Gore's campaign staff. There was some early tension between the VP's campaign staff and me, but ultimately it all worked out—however, not before some real drama at the Beverly Wilshire hotel the day of the speech.

Although most of the Tennessee convention delegation stayed at a downtown LA hotel near the Staples Center, I wanted to limit distractions before the speech, so I moved to the Beverly Wilshire. The morning of the speech I still hadn't settled on the final remarks. Levien and I had met at 4:00 A.M. to finish the remarks and integrate them into the campaign staff's remarks for me, which didn't really capture my voice. We worked until 1:00 P.M. with a few interruptions—three press calls and a call from the nominee himself. As soon as we finished, we decided to celebrate on the balcony off my suite with some high fives in the warm sun and glasses of sparkling water. I was still in my boxers, the hotel robe, and my black Nike high-tops. We placed the ten-page speech on the glass table on the balcony as we looked over the balcony and admired the scene at the pool six floors down. All of a sudden, a soft and refreshing LA wind gust lifted five pages of my speech about six feet in the air off the table and neatly blew them over my balcony rail onto the balcony of the room to our left. It all happened so fast that we had no time to react and try to grab the papers as they were in flight.

Levien wanted to try to jump to the next balcony—from

six floors up—because he feared the papers would fly off the other balcony in seconds. "J Love, don't do it," I said, using Levien's nickname. He came to his senses, and we quickly ran through the room and out my door to knock on the door of my neighbors. No one answered. We were worrying for many reasons, most urgently because we didn't have a copy of what we had written. "We have one copy. We have to get in this room," I said to the confused-looking housekeeper in the hall. She eventually capitulated and opened the door and escorted me onto the balcony. Levien had gone back onto my balcony to make sure none of the other pages had flown anywhere else. I grabbed the pages from the neighboring balcony and ran back to my room.

Levien, who was still wearing his clothes from the day before, collected the speech and gave it one more read. He left the hotel and rushed to the Staples Center to get it to the convention team so they could put it in the teleprompter. We could have faxed it, but I wanted Levien there to make sure they didn't alter the remarks too much. He got there in time. I delivered the speech late that evening. This moment helped make me a national figure in the Democratic Party.

IN 2002, HOUSE Democrats were again optimistic about our chances to win (back) the majority. Bin Laden had not been found, deficits were growing again, and the middle class was ever more worried about their financial security, especially after the collapses of Enron and WorldCom and the ensuing corporate accounting scandals.

After our loss that year, there was great disappointment throughout the Democratic caucus and widespread criticism, in private, of the leadership. The day after the election, I went on *CBS Evening News* with Bob Schieffer and raised the possibility of Democrats needing new leadership. I promised that if Dick Gephardt sought reelection, he would face opposition. I knew of no candidate, but I had consulted with a dozen or so Democratic colleagues about the election results and the possibility of a change in leadership. And I was prepared to challenge Gephardt if no one emerged.

Running against Gephardt, who was both well-respected and well-liked, would be a steep challenge. It would likely cause upheaval in important political circles in Washington. But I had sat on the back benches for three terms, and I was tired of just questioning the leadership's strategy to no avail. I wanted to be more proactive. I wanted to give the caucus an opportunity to vote for something new. Ordinarily, no one challenged the leadership, but I knew the status quo was no longer acceptable for me or my constituents. Republicans had screwed the country up, and the House Democratic leadership had tried to stop it but couldn't. We needed change. Win or lose, I was prepared to try to deliver that change. Democratic constituencies across the country were depending on us to develop public policy that would make the country stronger, smarter, healthier, and safer.

On the Thursday after the election, Gephardt announced that he would not seek reelection to the minority leader's post, acknowledging that it was time for fresh leadership in the House. It was the honorable thing to do. It unleashed a frenzy of political jockeying. Nancy Pelosi and Martin Frost had been vying for the position of minority whip—the second highest Democrat in leadership. They both jumped to the minority leader's race.

Frost had been trailing Pelosi in the whip race, and it quickly became clear that he wouldn't make up the distance in a race for minority leader. I started to consider the race seriously at that moment. I knew that Frost, whom I had been supporting for minority whip, was having problems persuading many of the progressive members to support him. I knew that Pelosi would be a formidable opponent. She was smart, wealthy, and as persuasive a one-on-one campaigner as there was in Congress, and her base encompassed nearly the entire California delegation—the biggest in the Democratic caucus—women, and progressives.

My thinking was that a bloc of Blue Dog, New Democrat, Hispanic, and Congressional Black Caucus members could deliver me a narrow victory. My model was similar to a coalition put together almost two decades earlier by former Democratic whip Bill Gray, the first African American to hold a leadership position in the House.

I decided to announce for the leadership race in Memphis, but I wanted a national platform to do it. My best friend in the national media at the time was Don Imus. And his national radio platform, which was televised on MSNBC, was a format I had been on and felt comfortable on. And I knew Don was enough of a contrarian to at least find the idea interesting. At best, he might even support me. His endorsement would be huge for me. Imus and I hadn't coordinated before I went on the show that Friday morning, so I didn't know what his response would be. Imus endorsed me.

After making the announcement, I immediately flew back to D.C. to begin the campaign in earnest. It would require a tremendous amount of work. I needed to call every one of my Democratic colleagues and then contact all the newly elected House Democrats. I also decided to do as much national press as I could. Although my congressional colleagues comprised the voting constituency, I needed to excite Democrats around the country about the prospect of change.

The calls started to flood my congressional offices from supportive Democrats nationally. The online support ramped up considerably. Old friends and new friends came to my support. My old and dear friend Alfred Liggins, who owns radio stations nationally, provided me a platform on some of his stations in Detroit, Washington, D.C., Chicago, and Baltimore to make my case for the leadership position. And I received support from new friends, like Justin Dangel, who started an online effort to help get me elected. The case made by Justin mirrored mine—Democrats needed to change if we wanted to win a majority.

My top aide, Mark Schuermann, organized the day-to-day team. Friends and former staffers flew in from across the country. My former chief of staff, Jarvis Stewart, arrived to handle K Street outreach. My dad flew up from Memphis. Longtime friends Daniel Halpern and Charles Robert Bone flew in from out of town. My college classmate Annalise Carol, who was then working at a big public relations firm in New York City, flew in to help with press without telling me. She saw the news, packed a bag, and hopped on a plane. She didn't have a place to stay when she left, but on Friday morning, she was in the office, ready to manage my media relations and political outreach operations. And then longtime Democratic operative Lanny Davis, who had once been my boss at Patton, Boggs, joined us to lend a hand. He was the first Washington operative to support me publicly.

We knew the odds were long, but we went at it nonstop for five days. I worked the phones hard, talking with any House colleague who would take my call. The press followed the race closely; in the span of a few days, I appeared on every political cable and network show, including NBC's *Nightly News* and ABC's *This Week*.

Ironically, Dick Gephardt had given me my campaign theme when he acknowledged that Democrats needed "fresh leadership." I contended that the country deserved much better than anything the Republicans had offered. Just two years after Clinton's successful stewardship of the nation's economy, Americans again distrusted Democrats on taxes and deficit spending. Voters also distrusted us on national security. For the good of the country, we needed to craft new policies on taxes, education, and national security. I urged tax cuts for small businesses, more education funding for states that embraced reform, a return to the fiscal discipline that President Clinton had introduced, and a renewed, open-ended commitment to finding Osama bin Laden, dead or alive.

Politically, I believed that a Democratic majority would only come if we won more Republican districts, whose voters were worried about deficits, jobs, high energy prices, and terrorism. Democrats in Washington needed to recruit candidates who truly fit the districts in which they were running, not some national Democratic agenda. As my friend and fellow congressman John Tanner often used to say, "The only vote Washington Democrats should be worried about from congressional Democrats is the vote for Speaker." Translation: Let moderate and conservative Democrats run their own campaigns and win. Then let them vote for a Democrat for Speaker. This was my message to the Democratic caucus—with one important kicker. I promised that I would serve only one term if I couldn't produce a majority by 2004. I challenged Pelosi to make the same pledge. She never did.

To my surprise, very few of my colleagues disagreed with me about the need for fresh Democratic leadership and a new strategy to defeat the Republicans. Many told me that they would consider voting for me. Other colleagues said that they had fully committed to Pelosi and worried about political retribution if they switched their votes, but they nonetheless supported my campaign platform. Still other colleagues told me that I was nuts to be challenging the leadership.

The race was Thursday, November 14. I was nominated by my fellow Tennessee colleague John Tanner; fellow Blue Dog member Charlie Stenholm of Texas; William Clay, Jr., of Missouri; Brad Carson of Oklahoma; Adam Smith of Washington; and Denise Majette of Georgia. The vote—177–29 for Pelosi—didn't go my way, but I was pleased that many of my Blue Dog colleagues had supported me. I lost badly among Congressional Black Caucus members. The CBC's opposition was hurtful because I had grown up with and around them. I didn't expect automatic support because of race, but I certainly didn't expect the vitriolic opposition that some directed toward my candidacy. On another level, the CBC opposition, mostly from veteran CBC members, was hypocritical because so many of them had been elected to Congress by challenging an unresponsive establishment. Now many were opposing me for doing what they all had done. They had become the establishment.

I was disappointed with the outcome. But my run for leadership had three additional and unintended effects, and all three were positive. First, the race changed the way House Democrats conducted politics and policy. My campaign led to a broad recognition within the caucus that we could not win a majority by targeting only liberal voters. To win a majority, Democrats would have to take the fight to moderate-to-conservative districts. Second, my campaign emboldened rank-and-file members to dissent more openly when the leadership's policy directives were counterproductive. And finally, the leadership race fully established me as a pro-business and moderate Democratic voice within the party. And that could only help in the long term. I was still learning.

MAKING THEM WHOLE

I FLEW INTO BAGRAM AIR BASE FOR THE FIRST TIME ON February 29, 2002. We had overnighted in Tashkent, Uzbekistan, because it was too unsafe to stay in Afghanistan. The sheer beauty of the country surprised me. Gorgeous snow-topped mountains extended to the horizon. If you didn't know where you were, you could easily have believed you were in the American West, flying over the Wasatch Mountains in Utah or the Rockies in Colorado.

I was traveling with a congressional delegation led by David Hobson, an influential Republican congressman from Ohio. We were among an early group of congresspeople visiting the country after the attacks of 9/11. I had gone because I thought a visit would deepen my understanding of the new threats to our country. As a legislator, I needed to be able to help shape intelligent responses to those threats.

What I was after was greater insight. I knew that visiting the commanders and troops on the ground was essential. Having listened to Donald Rumsfeld and Paul Wolfowitz in committee hearings, I surmised that there was a disconnect between the rhetoric at home and the reality on the ground. Seeing the situation firsthand was the only way to understand what it meant to prosecute the Afghanistan war the right way. Between my first trip to Afghanistan and my last days in office, I visited Iraq and Afghanistan at least once a year, and my experience helped form my opinions and gave me credibility at home to offer alternatives to what we were doing on the ground in Afghanistan, and ultimately in Iraq.

On my first day at the Bagram Air Base, we drove in a heavily fortified vehicle from the base as a part of a motorcade to the American embassy in Kabul. It was in the heart of the city, which looked like a bustling third-world bazaar. We pulled up to the grounds of the embassy and found ourselves looking up at a fortified compound. To get inside, we had to pass through three different security checkpoints and four huge gates.

When we finally made it through security and walked into the embassy, we were met by the stench of urine. It was overwhelming at first. I eventually acclimated.

We went upstairs and met with a group of senior military officers. They apologized for the conditions. "We're working on getting better facilities," one of them said, "but right now this is the best we have." Our chief diplomatic officer in Afghanistan at the time, Ryan Crocker, explained later that there were only two bathrooms in the entire embassy. One was reserved for Crocker and his wife, but they let everybody use it. All the military and the State Department personnel worked there. The conditions were tough.

Ambassador Crocker told us that the United States had

pushed the Taliban out of the city very quickly and proven that we could control Kabul; but the Taliban controlled many of the outer provinces, and we didn't yet have the manpower or resources to counter them.

Crocker then turned to the need for more money for civil engineering projects. I didn't appreciate the magnitude of the infrastructure challenges at first. But it quickly became apparent. The country was completely devastated. Roads, schools, hospitals, bridges—it needed everything. The budget for the engineering projects was inadequate. It was obvious that more money was needed. We had nowhere near the funding necessary to extend meaningful infrastructure into the provinces. Congressman Hobson, whose committee controlled spending, promised that Congress would help.

Crocker was smart and impressive. He was honest about the political and military challenges facing the United States. He spoke about the skepticism from Afghans, the doubts about our intentions, the fragility of Afghanistan's leadership, and the great difficulty of creating a functioning government. Afghanistan would need an army willing to fight insurgents and a police force capable of protecting the population. It was becoming increasingly clear that the war was going to consume vast resources—military, civilian, and political.

"Chairman Karzai's challenges are real," Crocker said, before making clear that he believed we could achieve our goals in Afghanistan—it was just going to take time.

We told Crocker we wanted to go out and see the city, and he arranged an escort. We pulled out of the compound in armored SUVs and drove to a nearby hospital. It was horrible—

dirty, completely unsanitary, and overcrowded. There were eight or ten people to a room. They had limited medical supplies, and the waiting and treatment rooms were germ incubators.

We then drove to a school roughly thirty minutes outside of Kabul. We were carrying letters that American schoolchildren had written to Afghan schoolchildren, and we were going to deliver them to the Afghan students.

On our way to the school, we passed an open-air marketplace, a traditional bazaar, and there was a welcome aliveness to the place. People were haggling over prices and socializing, and they seemed comfortable. The Taliban may have had a presence in the area, but it was a far smaller presence, I assumed, than it had been before our military controlled Kabul. My group was encouraged. This seemed like a small but meaningful victory over chaos—a modest return to normalcy in a country that had been at war for more than two decades.

But when I asked if we could stop and walk through the market, one of our American armed guards said, flatly, "No, we're not stopping." I said, "Why not?" He said, "It looks safe, but it's not. If we stop the car and get out, insurgents will come out of nowhere, and we'll have a problem. There aren't enough of us to guard you." It was a sobering illustration of the tenuous security situation. The scene looked perfectly peaceful and harmless, but that illusion greeted me over and over in Afghanistan.

The school's physical condition was as bad as the hospital's; it was dirty and overcrowded and smelled of urine. The kids, though, couldn't have been nicer. Their positive spirit matched that of their teachers, and that of the doctors and patients at the hospital. I was learning.

ONE OF THE striking things about these trips was how quickly we moved among countries and between levels of society. On visits to Afghanistan, we would stay in surrounding cities and commute by air into and out of Kabul. During my first trip, the day after we delivered our letters to the Afghan kids in the squalid school, we found ourselves on an Uzbek military base, toasting a joint-use agreement with Russian generals. Hobson had been involved in the talks because of his committee, so he signed some ceremonial paperwork to seal the deal.

This happened at ten thirty in the morning. The Russian generals wanted us to toast the deal with vodka shots. I thought, "There's no way I'm having a shot of vodka." We were all try-ing to stay on American time. The schedule was so tight that we never got more than three or four hours of sleep a night, and we had to hit the ground running whenever we landed. The idea was for us to get as much sleep as possible on the way over and on all the plane rides during the trip and fight our way through the sleep deprivation. As we were sitting with the generals, I leaned over and said to Hobson, "If I have a shot, I'm not going to be able to walk the rest of the day."

"You have to have a shot," Hobson said. "This is what they do. We don't want to offend anyone."

Tradition was tradition, so I took the shot. It was pure raw Russian vodka—moonshine, we would call it in Tennessee. I was useless the rest of that day.

The highlights of this first trip were our meetings and discussions with U.S. soldiers and commanders and our meeting with President Karzai. The courage and sacrifice of our soldiers and their families was stunning. Equally remarkable and sad was how we as a nation treated soldiers, military families, and veterans. We didn't pay our soldiers sufficiently, and didn't ensure that their families were adequately protected and cared for while they served. We didn't even guarantee that returning soldiers would get the health care they needed.

I will never forget having dinner on Bagram with a Tennessee soldier and learning this firsthand. I could barely see what I was eating. There were no lights on at the base because the pilots were flying their missions at night. Even the mess hall was without electric lights. We ate by candlelight. The young man I was sitting next to was attached to the Tennessee National Guard. He was from Jackson, Tennessee. He was in his late thirties, and in civilian life he worked as a golf equipment salesman.

He said, "Don't worry. You came on a good night. It's pasta night."

I said, "Is that right?"

He said, "It's lasagna tonight."

We went on to have a great conversation. He loved the work he was doing and had no concerns about the nature of the mission. What did concern him—what concerned many of our National Guard soldiers—was the financial strain his deployment was placing on his family.

"I'm probably going to lose my job," he said. "I'm not getting paid. My wife's working, but I'm really worried about her. It's tough on her. I was making $75,000 a year, and I just lost my salary. That's the part of this situation I have a problem with. We're doing a longer tour than we normally would. I know I have a job to do here, and I'm willing to do it, but it's hurting my family." The amazing thing to me was that more soldiers in his position didn't quit—that they didn't just say, "I'm going AWOL. I'm going back home to work. I want to serve my country, but I have to take care of my family."

After dinner, walking to the SUV that would take us to the runway, I was saying to myself, "How can we treat our soldiers this way?"

It was freezing outside. In Afghanistan, it was warm during the day and cold at night. I remember looking up at the sky, seeing flares and hearing fighter jets streaking. I could see explosions in the distance. The Taliban was exchanging fire with our soldiers, and I could see the tracer arcs in the night sky.

We were moving quickly in the SUVs—with our lights off. I was sitting behind the driver, a young Marine. He had the window down. After three or four minutes, I was freezing. I said, "Soldier, you mind putting that window up a little bit?"

He said, "Sir, I wish I could. I can't. We don't have our lights on, so I need the window down. I need to feel the heat from the car in front of me to know where I'm going."

I said, "All right. Can I ask you a question? How does the guy in front of you know where he's going?"

"Sir, he does the same thing I'm doing. He has his window down, too, and is being led by the SUV in front of him."

"How about the guy in front of him?"

"Sir, he does the same thing."

"What about the guy in front?"

"Sir, my job is to follow the guy in front of me. I don't know what the lead guy does. I just follow orders."

I had the distinct impression that he wanted to say, "Look, motherf—er, that's not my damn job! My job is to follow this guy in front of me, and that's what I'm doing!" But he was very respectful.

I was sitting there thinking, "This is how you have to live when you're fighting a war. If you don't follow orders, you die." This soldier wasn't worried about how the guy at the head of the convoy was navigating. It was not on his mind. His job was to follow the vehicle in front of him. That was a great lesson for me. You follow the plan. You trust and follow orders. That's how you survive and win in war.

I said, "I understand, soldier."

MY FIRST TRIP to Iraq and the Middle East was in mid-August 2003. I traveled with a Senate delegation led by John McCain. Senators John Sununu, Kay Bailey Hutchison, Lindsey Graham, and Maria Cantwell were also on the trip. I was the only House member on the trip. We first traveled to Israel and the West Bank, visiting holy sites and meeting with Prime Minister Ariel Sharon.

Baghdad was far more tense than Kabul because the U.S. military didn't control Baghdad like it did Kabul. In Iraq, we spent all of our time in the Green Zone. To get from the Baghdad airport to the Green Zone, we went by helicopter. The highway from the Baghdad airport to the Green Zone was too dangerous.

I was fortunate enough to meet up on more than one occasion in Iraq with then senator Joe Biden, who traveled to Iraq more than any member of Congress. His questions in meetings were always the most thoughtful and pointed. And Biden also helped me pack and dress for these trips. I remember him explaining late one night after a long day of meetings:

> You bring gray slacks and a blazer and a cheap blue suit that you don't care about getting dirty. You wear the suit for meetings with political leaders. You bring two or three dress shirts. Keep one clean—you'll wear it when you have meetings with officials. You bring your shitkickers. You bring a pair of shorts, a workout T-shirt, and running shoes. And then you just fight through sleep because you won't get any while on the ground.

I followed Biden's advice on each subsequent trip. On the first trip with McCain, we met with military leaders including Lieutenant General Ricardo Sanchez, our commanding military officer on the ground, and with the U.S. civilian administrator, Paul Bremer. While meeting with Bremer and Sanchez in the Coalition Provisional Authority headquarters on that

first trip, my delegation learned that the United Nations offices in Baghdad had been bombed. The bombing claimed the
lives of dozens of U.N. workers, including the U.N.'s top Iraqi
envoy, Sérgio Vieira de Mello. Vieira de Mello was a U.N.
envoy who devoted his life to bringing peace to difficult circumstances. He was universally respected in diplomatic circles
around the globe. It was a sad day. After that bombing, the
U.N. never reopened the office.

On each of these Middle East trips, I made a point of walking around as much as I could. I wanted to get a feel for the
texture of life there. I wanted to understand the bases. I wanted
to see where the soldiers showered, where they ate, where they
went to the bathroom, and so forth. Most of the bathroom
facilities were outdoors. The arrangements were uncomfortable. You gain a real appreciation for the rigors of the day-to-
day life.

We would always get a briefing from the senior officers on
the Iraqi bases. The officers were impressive. Smart, tough,
and poised, all of them had nothing but positive outlooks in
the briefing. They always projected confidence in the mission.
Now, that's not to say that they weren't honest about a maturing and determined enemy force, especially as the insurgents
used more and more IEDs to kill our soldiers.

The most difficult thing for me to reconcile about Iraq was
that the world's greatest, most technologically equipped and
best-trained war fighters—the U.S. military—were confronting and being dealt a setback by an army of insurgents lacking
in technology, training, and numbers when compared to the
United States. Further, the insurgents were killing large num-

bers of our soldiers using an old detonator technology. We were using the latest iPods and HPs; they were using Walkmen and word processors. Something didn't make sense to me.

I started believing in late 2004 that maybe we needed more troops on the ground. Bush and Rumsfeld argued that the United States would put more troops on the ground in Iraq if the generals would ask. On each of my trips to Iraq, my delegation was always told that more troops would be terrific and likely helpful. "But we feel confident that we can achieve our mission with current troop levels," the generals would always conclude.

Privately, when the generals were asked, they were more direct in admitting the need for more troops.

I'd ask, "Do you need more troops?"

They would say, "Yes."

I'd ask, "Did you send a request to the administration?"

They'd say, "No."

I'd ask, "Why not?"

Their answer was that the civilian commanders at the Department of Defense didn't want to hear it. Rumsfeld didn't want to hear it. Commanders feared losing their jobs if they pressed Rumsfeld.

The enlisted men and women we talked to, despite being in the presence of their superiors, also spoke honestly. Many of them highlighted the same concern that Crocker had in Afghanistan in 2002: the need to provide more services like electricity and health care. There was a growing belief among officers and soldiers alike that the overall and long-term success of our efforts would be determined by how much we improved the quality of life for ordinary Iraqis—a lot like the message U.S. politicians deliver during election seasons.

One of the most interesting needs cited by General Ray Odierno during my trip to Iraq was for more Arabic translators. I was surprised. General Odierno, now our top general on the ground in Iraq, said that his communications with local tribal leaders in Tikrit was limited. He said, "I can't communicate well enough with local leaders. In any crowded meeting, I lose what's being said because one translator can't follow all the conversations around the room."

Again, the greatest military force in the world was handicapped in war because of . . . language. I was beginning to understand better the vast scope of challenges and perils facing our troops. And some of the challenges seemed straightforward if not simple.

The other chief predicament for the United States—one we're now facing in Afghanistan—was that we were often forced to partner with corrupt, tribally biased governments. By far the most fascinating meeting I took part in in Iraq was a dinner in January 2006—during my last trip to Iraq—at the home of the then president, Jalal Talabani. The delegation was led by Indiana senator Evan Bayh and included Senator Kit Bond and then senator Barack Obama. It was Barack's first trip to Iraq.

We arrived and had drinks at the president's home. None of the U.S. delegation had alcohol. But our Iraqi hosts, including other senior Iraqi political leaders and the infamous Ahmed Chalabi, enjoyed wine and Johnnie Walker Blue. Talabani couldn't have been more hospitable. The food, served buffet-style, was excellent.

Once we were seated for dinner, Chalabi made a proposal that he spent a good portion of the dinner elaborating on. It became apparent to the U.S. delegation that one of the central purposes of the dinner was to consider Chalabi's proposal for an Iraqi-run, U.S.-backed Fannie Mae–like organization in Iraq that would make home ownership a reality for a majority of Iraqis.

The answer to Iraq's problems, Chalabi believed, was home ownership! It was imperative, he argued, that America expand home ownership for Iraqis. The United States should fund it, and Chalabi would run it. He actually said this.

Barack was sitting directly across from me, and Chalabi was on Barack's side of the table. I caught Barack's eye for a moment; he half smiled and then looked over at Chalabi, incredulously. The whole thing was surreal.

I TRIED TO attend the funerals of soldiers from my district who were killed in Iraq or Afghanistan. I missed only a handful.

I rarely announced that I was coming. I would just show up, and sometimes the families were shocked to see me. I would arrive, sign the guestbook, and sit in the back of the church. Even when asked to sit up front, I politely refused.

I always carried an official congressional resolution recognizing the soldier's service and sacrifice. I would deliver it to the family after the service.

Usually, I didn't speak. Sometimes, family members would ask me to say something, and all I would ever say was "As your congressman, I want to thank you and your family for your sacrifice. Your nation can never repay you fully for your service to your country." And if appropriate, I would read part of the resolution.

The things said at these funerals about these young men and women were always profoundly touching. You sat and listened to people talk about their child, their brother, their grandchild, their student, or someone they coached. People talked about how great an athlete or student the person was, how funny he or she was, and how much he or she loved and was loved by his or her family and friends. The things people said about these young patriots humanized them. They all had something in common—love for their country and youth.

I don't recall ever going to the funeral of anybody over twenty-five years old. Most of the fallen soldiers had graduated from high school two or three years earlier. Usually, the soldier's entire family and community of friends attended the funerals, so you saw the scope of the soldiers' lives and realized how little they had lived and how much they were loved. The stories of their lives formed arcs. At funerals for young people, mourners talk about hope and ambition, about wonderful personal qualities that will never be fully enjoyed or appreciated, and about unrealized promise.

I vividly remember sitting in the back pews of all of these churches and listening to people illustrate the human toll of war, which helped me to understand even more what the senior military officers meant when they would say how much they hated war. And that wars should be employed only after great planning and thought. I was still learning.

MORE DAVIDS THAN
GOLIATHS

I T WAS OCTOBER OF 2005, STILL VERY EARLY IN MY SEN-
ate campaign, and I was out visiting churches in Jackson,
Tennessee. The day had been organized by Shirlene Mer-
cer, a district director for my colleague John Tanner. She was
also an old friend and a mentor. She set it up for me to visit one
of Jackson's largest black churches and meet its dynamic pastor, Bishop Nathaniel Bond.

When I arrived at his church, I was escorted to Bishop
Bond's private office. I was traveling with two other people—
John Freeman and Rashana Lincoln, both old friends who
were helping me in the campaign. Bishop Bond led us in prayer
after a short meeting and then whispered something to me as
we were about to exit his office to enter the sanctuary: "Remember two things as you go through this campaign: There
are more Davids than Goliaths, and more answers than problems." Bishop Bond was well aware that as an African American Democrat running in Tennessee, I would not have an easy
journey. His words stayed with me the rest of the day—and
campaign. It was a sentiment I hadn't heard expressed in a

while, and it reminded me of Pastor Payne's words during vacation Bible study. But there had to be a reason, I kept thinking, why Bishop Bond shared that piece of wisdom with me on this particular day. The Lord works in mysterious ways. I was convinced that another reason was apparent that I just hadn't seen yet.

It was terrific from start to finish that day. I was received warmly at each of the churches I visited. I felt good about what I was doing, despite the steep odds facing my campaign. My message was resonating with people. I wanted to connect with voters in Jackson like I had connected with voters in Memphis in 1996—in a very personal way. I needed to deconstruct some of the criticism coming my way and introduce myself to voters on my terms. I wanted voters to know that the portrait the press and my Democratic and Republican critics had drawn of me conflicted mightily with who I was, how and where I grew up, and the kind of public servant I wanted to be for the entire state of Tennessee. I left Jackson late that afternoon full of energy, hope, and optimism about our day and the campaign.

But I still had not witnessed the significance of what Bishop Bond had said, "There are more Davids than Goliaths." Then it hit me as John drove past a little roadside bar and burger joint called the Lil' Rebel on our way back to the interstate. The Lil' Rebel featured a big Confederate flag painted along its side, and another Confederate flag hung above its front door. There was also a Confederate flag on the small billboard that advertised to drivers passing by on the road.

I immediately thought of Bishop Bond's words, and something clicked. "You know what? I'm supposed to stop here. We need to turn around."

We had just driven past the bar. "You have to be kidding me," John, who is white, said as he looked over at me.

I said, "No. There's something about this place. We need to stop there. I heard something important in church earlier from Bishop Bond. There's a reason we need to stop. There are more Davids than Goliaths."

"You sure you want to do this?" John asked.

I said, "You know what? What's the worst thing that can happen?"

"Harold, the place is painted in Confederate flags," Rashana, who is black, firmly reminded me.

"Look, if anybody says anything to us, we're just going to turn around and walk out. Okay?" John admonished.

I said, "All right. We'll just walk out. But work with me here. They may like me," I said nervously.

John turned around and pulled into the small parking lot at the Lil' Rebel. There were six or seven parked cars, a majority of which had NRA and George W. Bush bumper stickers on them. My nervousness grew. There was no way to know how we were going to be received. I had Bishop Bond's words in my mind, though, and I just believed that there was a reason to stop.

We walked in. The place was small but crowded. It smelled like cheeseburgers and fries. On the walls were Confederate flags, pinup girl calendars, the season's NASCAR schedule, and beer signs. Pool balls clacked on a table in the back.

The patrons turned around and looked at us—at me mainly. I introduced myself and said I'd been on the road campaigning and wanted to stop in and say hello. No one said anything for a moment, and then a pretty woman sitting at the bar smiled at me.

"Sweetheart, we've been waiting on you to stop by," she said warmly. She was about five feet three, dressed in jeans and a T-shirt. She walked over, opened up her arms, and gave me a big hug. "This is amazing," she said. "There's a guy comes in here every day who's always talking about you. The one day you decide to stop by, he doesn't come."

"He talks about how smart you are, and how you should be judged on your merits and no one else's, and how good a senator you'd be. Man, he's going to be mad he's not here," said a guy sitting at the bar.

I was shocked. The embrace was warm. The bartender invited me to put my bumper sticker—which said "Jr. for Senate"—on his refrigerator door, which featured dozens of NASCAR driver stickers. Rashana chatted it up with some patrons in the back of the bar and even started playing pool. John ordered us cheeseburgers to go—even though we had just eaten pork shoulder and ribs at Shirlene's.

Then my campaign instincts really kicked in. Everyone was so friendly I immediately asked if I could put my campaign bumper stickers on all the cars and trucks in the parking lot. My dad would be proud.

They said yes, so I went outside and got to work. I enjoyed putting my sticker right above the "W. for President" bumper stickers.

The man who lived next door to the Lil' Rebel was sitting on his porch, and he saw me putting bumper stickers on the cars and pickups. A big POW-MIA flag was draped over his porch railing. He parked his car, it turned out, in the Lil' Rebel lot. And I was about to sticker his car.

When he yelled, "Don't you put a damn bumper sticker on my damn car," the manager of the Lil' Rebel, who had come out with me, called the guy over to meet me. He walked over gingerly, using a cane. He was wearing a pair of dark khakis, a light blue shirt with suspenders, and a POW-MIA hat. He walked right up to me and poked at my chest as he talked. I remember it like it was yesterday.

"I don't like politicians," he said. "I don't trust politicians. None of them are any good. All they do is spend other people's money." He continued poking me insistently. "What are you gonna do if you get elected?" he asked.

I said jokingly, "Well, first I'll do whatever it takes to get you to stop hitting me in my chest."

He smiled and stopped. It was actually hurting, so I was glad he did.

"Look," I continued, "I share your concerns about politicians. But I can tell you that I'm not like most of them. If you've been listening to what my opponents are saying about me, you might know that I'm different from just about anyone who has run in Tennessee before."

He chuckled a bit.

"If you send me up there," I said, "and I don't do right by you, then send me back home. But give me a shot to go up there and try to fix things. I think you're right. Politicians do spend too much money. They tell you they're going to do things they don't do, and the next time they see you, they act like they did them. But I have a funny feeling you won't let me do that. I won't come back here and ask for your vote again if I haven't delivered on what I promised."

He looked halfway persuaded. "All right, go ahead and put a bumper sticker on my car." I did, with all the care my father had taught me. I shook hands with everyone and then got into the car and headed back to Memphis.

Bishop Bond was right, I thought.

The experience emboldened me even more to go everywhere in the state. The campaign strategy was simple: get out and touch as many people as I could. The patrons of the Lil' Rebel validated the approach. The people of Tennessee were better, I knew, than the press and top political thinkers suggested. Much like the people who had called in to the radio show during my first congressional race, the Lil' Rebel patrons were listening to me and decided to give me a chance. On the way back to Memphis, I said to John, "We have to keep doing this. We can't stop working. We can't ever let up. If we stay at this race like we did today, we can win."

TWO OR THREE weeks later, I had just finished speaking at a dinner for the local Democratic Party in Martin, Tennessee, when a man approached and asked if he could have a word with me. He was a thin guy, probably in his mid-fifties. I was in a hurry to leave because I had to make another campaign stop forty or fifty miles away—and it was late. I said, "Yes, sir.

Can you talk to me as we walk out? I have another event and I'm going to have to jump in the car and go." I wanted to hear what he had to say.

I thought he just wanted to take a picture or offer some words of encouragement. He waited as I shook hands and hugged people, and when we got to the door, he said, "Let me ask you something. Did you stop by the Lil' Rebel a couple weeks ago?" It hit me as soon as he said it—this must be the regular at the Lil' Rebel who hadn't been there the day I visited.

I said, "You're John. You're the guy who wasn't there that day."

"Yeah! How'd you know?" he asked.

We gave each other a hug, and he said,

You don't know the impact you made on those people at the Lil' Rebel. You won all of them over, and they're all gonna talk about you to everybody who comes in. Every time you see one of those places, stop. That's your only chance to win this race. You're gonna be surprised at the number of people who'll vote for you if you just stop and see them. When people meet you, they're going to like you. I don't know you, but I was telling all of them that the more they listen to you, the more they'll like you. You got to do that everywhere in the state. I mean everywhere.

I said, "Yes, sir," and thanked him for supporting me so vocally at the Lil' Rebel. Then I let the windows down in the SUV and yelled out, "I hope you keep helping me."

"Believe me," he yelled back, "I'm helping you everywhere I can."

I told the Lil' Rebel story at virtually every campaign stop. I remember telling it at a Democratic Party picnic in Henry Horton State Park, in Chapel Hill, Tennessee, about six months later. I told the crowd that I wasn't afraid to take the campaign anywhere and that so far I had been embraced everywhere. After I finished the speech, I was working the crowd and shaking hands, and a guy walked up to me and said, "Young man, I own a place like the Lil' Rebel except we don't serve alcohol. I want you to come by and see us. We'll treat you well, and I bet people will take to you. We have a pool table too. The only problem is, we don't have a Confederate flag up. But if it'll make you feel more comfortable, I'll rush right back and put one up tonight." Everyone within earshot laughed, and I promised him I'd stop by. And I did late that evening.

INITIALLY, THE PEOPLE I had the most trouble convincing of my electability were other loyal Tennessee Democrats. My Democratic governor, Phil Bredesen, had doubts, my Tennessee congressional colleagues publicly and privately expressed reservations about me, and most Tennessee Democratic Party activists worried out loud that I was the wrong candidate.

A lot of their worry, though by no means all of it, had to do with race. From the outset of the campaign, I knew that race would be an issue. It was on the minds of everyone who thought about me, the Senate, and Tennessee. Many of my earliest and fiercest supporters did not think Tennesseans would elect a black senator, and my opponents were counting on them not to. I refused to accept the premise that race would stop me from winning. My belief was that it would become almost irrelevant given Tennesseans' intense frustration with their lives and government's inaction on an agenda to make things better. The state's voters were facing lackluster job growth, two poorly managed wars, and a growing national debt exacerbated by the extravagant spending of a Republican president. Tennesseans, I thought, were suffering more from the wars and the weak economy than most. Ultimately, I believed, they would vote for change in Washington.

Beyond race, everyone knew that the Republicans would try to characterize me as an extreme liberal without a moral nucleus and as an outsider, a spoiled kid who had grown up in Washington and then served for ten years in Congress. There was no way, they would claim, that I could understand Tennessee values.

The Democratic Party establishment's opposition deepened my resolve because I believed the party—and the country—was in need of a different kind of leadership. I thought Tennessee voters would respond positively to a fiscally conservative Democrat who shared many of their values. Furthermore, I believed the timing was right. Nationally, voters were worried that our dependence on oil would continue to weaken our homeland security. George Bush and the Republicans were more at fault than Democrats. And I was a fiscally responsible Democrat. I believed I could take advantage of that sentiment in Tennessee. And win.

For a long time, southern Republicans had successfully

caricatured Democrats as morally out of touch with the main-stream of the country. They succeeded largely because most Democrats seemed afraid to attack the caricature and talk openly about faith and security. I refused to let that happen to me. Having attended church for as long as I could remember, I was not going to allow Republicans to undermine my candidacy on the grounds that I lacked a moral compass. I would aggressively and honestly enumerate the facts about me and faith. I grew up in church. I learned the difference between right and wrong—my parents taught it, and my grandmother and church reinforced it.

But I knew that the Republicans would continue to try to paint me as being out of touch with Tennessee, and they would use faith to whip up on me. They would make a concerted effort to portray me as out of touch with Tennessee. They wanted to raise doubts about me, even in the minds of traditional Democratic voters. It was a shrewd tactic by the Republicans, who took to calling me "Fancy Ford."

I had enjoyed great educational opportunities, I had a loving and supportive family, and I had been elected to Congress ten years earlier in a district facing significant social and economic challenges. The great irony was that of all the candidates running for Senate, I had the fewest assets. In fact, my eventual Republican opponent wrote a $12 million check to his own campaign.

But as much as race was front and center, there was another big issue. Less than twenty-four hours after I announced for the U.S. Senate, the FBI indicted and arrested my uncle

John, a long-serving state senator, on corruption charges. It wasn't the start I envisioned.

I HAD NO idea that my uncle was even being investigated by the FBI. His indictment was the culmination of a longtime FBI sting operation targeting politicians in the Tennessee state legislature. This was, to say the least, a strange turn of emotions and events. I got the news from my chief of staff, Mark Schuermann, as I was driving to my congressional office in Washington that morning.

We had scheduled a series of press briefings that day. I was going to discuss my immediate campaign plans and continue hammering away at Bush for his mishandling of the war in Iraq. I would then leave for Memphis early that afternoon to speak at a high school graduation. But a different set of facts defined the day and determined my schedule.

"Your uncle John has been arrested as a part of a federal sting operation," Mark told me. "You've got to be kidding!" I yelled into the phone. "What did they arrest him for?" Mark said he would find out more and call me back. When he did, several minutes later, he had the director of the Memphis FBI office on the line. She had been assigned to the job a few months earlier. We had met recently at a homeland security conference I sponsored in Memphis.

"Congressman, I wanted you to hear it from me," she said. "We just arrested your uncle, Senator John Ford, in Nashville, on multiple charges of bribery and corruption. He was implicated in a federal sting operation." She explained that he stood accused of taking bribes from businessmen seeking favorable treatment in the state. "I wish I could have told you about this before the arrest," she said, "but the ongoing nature of the investigation precluded me from discussing it. I'm sure you understand."

"I do," I said. "Thank you for your call, Madam Director." I'm not a conspiracy theory guy. But it was very curious to me that President Bush would appoint Memphis's first black FBI office director fewer than ninety days before my uncle was indicted. And she would be the one to phone and inform me of John's indictment. And all of this would happen the day after I announced for the Senate.

The next several hours, I knew, were critical. My initial response to the arrest would determine whether my campaign survived or not. Some of the first people I talked to advised me to fold right away. "You can't survive this kind of stress at the start of an already hard uphill fight," a Tennessee confidant said. A congressional colleague from middle Tennessee said it was "pretty much over" for my campaign. "I don't see how you recover from this," he told me on the House floor later that morning.

Although I was shaken by the turn of events, the thought of quitting never crossed my mind. My thinking remained what it had been from the outset: This was going to be an unconventional campaign. It had just gotten that much more unconventional.

I flew home that afternoon to speak at a high school graduation in East Memphis. With a little skill and a lot of prayer, I was able to avoid the media at the airport. I wanted to answer questions about my uncle while at work at a congressional event in the district. I did not want to give the impression that my uncle's arrest had disrupted my congressional or campaign schedule. It did, though.

I arrived at the graduation discreetly and greeted the headmaster and faculty. They acted as if nothing had happened, so I did, too. The program began. It was like any other graduation: parents giddily taking pictures as their kids entered the church sanctuary and students smiling as they received their diplomas. I stood with the headmaster and the chaplain at the front of the church. I spotted my old and dear friend Al Gossett in the audience. Al's niece was graduating that day. He winked at me, and I knew that the wink meant, "Hang in there, my friend." Walking out after the ceremony, I made it only halfway down the steps before reporters surrounded me. They interrupted one another as they shouted questions: "What are your thoughts about your uncle being arrested?" "What impact will the arrest have on you and your campaign for the Senate?" "Will you stay in the Senate race?"

I composed myself and addressed them.

Today is a difficult day for my family and me, but an even more challenging and confusing day for voters all across this state. They place their confidence in their elected officials. They expect honesty, integrity, and adherence to the law, and today they are disappointed.

I was blessed to be able to enter public service ten years ago. I grew up watching and learning from my father, who showed me the best side of politics and public service. Today, I stand here as a candidate for the United States Senate, asking the voters to judge me by who I am, what I have done, and what I will do if I am elected to the Senate. I want nothing more than to make life better for the citizens of this state. I trust that my uncle will soon get a fair hearing before a jury of his peers—and fully answer these charges. Until then, all I can do is serve the constituents of my district and ask voters across this great state to give me an opportunity to introduce myself and my ideas for making Tennessee and the nation strong.

The press screamed more questions at me, but that was all I was going to say on the matter that evening. I didn't want to speak again about my uncle but I knew I would have to. The next big statewide political event was the annual Tennessee Democratic Party dinner in Nashville. The Jackson Day Dinner, as it is known, attracted the party's key activists and biggest financial donors. Because we had a popular Democratic governor who would be on the ballot in 2006, it would also attract a lot of the Tennessee business class.

The angst about my candidacy burgeoned after my uncle's indictment. Although no one else had entered the Democratic primary—it was June 2005, more than ten months before the filing deadline—the party hierarchy was decidedly not coalescing around me. Talk about finding another candidate started to gain momentum. My governor didn't have favorable things to say about me—and neither did the Democratic congressional delegation.

I needed some encouragement. On the drive from Memphis to Nashville for the Jackson Day Dinner, I got a call from my dear friend Mellody Hobson. Mel and I had met in September 2000. Smart, sweet, and successful, Mel was a friend. Hearing her voice lifted my spirits. "Keep your chin up," she said. "You didn't do anything wrong, and you have nothing to be ashamed of. Fight through this moment with courage and dignity, and remember what Churchill said about dealing with adversity: 'When facing hard times, put your head down and charge through it until you get to the end of it.' It's the only way to get through these things." Her words of encouragement inspired me. They got me through the evening and the weeks after that. I quoted her in my speech that evening at Jackson Day.

The dinner was held outside, under a tent, in ninety-degree heat. The conditions muted the enthusiasm of the crowd. Each speaker got little more than polite applause.

When it was my turn to take the stage, I was nervous—like I had been going into the Lil' Rebel. I said, "I know there are some in this state, in Washington, and maybe even under this tent, who would love nothing more than to see me quit this Senate race because of who I am related to. But I am not a quitter."

The crowd started to cheer.

"I have spent ten years in Congress standing up for voters in my district," I went on. "I have worked to make schools better, to help businesses compete more effectively, to create jobs, and to keep America safe from those who would do us harm. I have sided with Republicans and President Bush when they were right, which is less and less often these days, and I have fought them vigorously when they were wrong. If you make me your nominee and elect me to the U.S. Senate, I will continue working every day to live up to your expectations and make Tennessee and America better and stronger for all of us."

I then used the Churchill quote I got from Mellody, and it electrified the crowd. I ended by saying, "Sometimes we are all disappointed by our families, but we love them, and we never run from them. All I ask is that you judge me by what I can control, and not by what I can't." The crowd erupted.

That evening rejuvenated my campaign. It affirmed that the best way to tackle my uncle's indictment was head-on. "Don't deal with this by doing phone interviews," my dad counseled, "and don't hide from anyone or shy away from answering tough questions. That's the only way you'll know whether you can overcome this thing." That's what I did. I spent the next few weeks traveling from one end of the state to the other with my chief travel deputy, Matt Reel, meeting with every newspaper's editorial board and answering every question anyone wanted to ask.

"WE SHOULD DO it—we should make the ad now," my campaign manager, Michael Powell, said. It was early 2006, and a national controversy had erupted. The Bush administration had agreed to outsource security at six major U.S. ports, including Baltimore, Miami, and New York, to a government-run company from Dubai. Powell and I were considering running an ad about it that criticized Bush for making this decision. Both Democrats and Republicans vehemently opposed the outsourcing. We couldn't understand why the Bush administration would give security control of our ports to a country that had given haven to the 9/11 terrorists. I had visited the Miami Port Authority and discussed port operations with senior personnel there. They were confused by the Bush administration's decision to outsource this security responsibility to a foreign government.

"This is bad for everyone," a senior official at the port said. "I don't see how we can do our jobs if we are not completely confident that our boss shares our commitment to safety." I understood. There were not alone in their worry.

"The ad can be up and running very soon," Powell said. "It's the right position to take, and the ad will convey clearly to Republicans that you're a serious candidate."

I had made the strategic decision to run ads early. We were eight months out. It was unusual to run an ad this soon. I had actually run an ad in July 2005. It was a patriotic Fourth of July ad thanking our soldiers for their service and sacrifice. It wasn't a huge ad buy—just enough to get everyone's attention. But, I continually needed to prove my seriousness and viability. The port security ads would be the first ads of the 2006 campaign cycle. I knew that every local and national news outlet would pick up on the ads and cover the campaign. It would demonstrate our seriousness.

The problem was that some in my party, particularly the head of the Democratic Senatorial Campaign Committee (DSCC), were opposed to my early spending. Chuck Schumer, the chairman of the DSCC, wanted me to raise my money and then hold it until much later in the campaign. But Schumer's thinking was conventional, and my campaign was unconventional. As the campaign unfolded, donors needed to see that I was competitive—that I could win. I would likely be unopposed in the Democratic primary, but the Republican primary would be fiercely contested and heavily covered. Waiting until after the primary to spend on TV ads would prove disastrous for me, I believed. In many ways, the Republican primary would be a contest to see who was the purest conservative, and I could not afford to be absent while the terms of the debate were being set. I could either spend early, establish my identity firmly as a Tennessee Democrat, and try to shift the debate in my favor; or I could wait, get defined by the Republicans, and then try to dig out in the twelve weeks left in the race after the primary. I bet on spending early.

Additionally, I knew Republicans would attack me for being weak on defense. As they did with every Democrat, they would try to label me a dove on national security. A well-done ad would begin the security conversation on my terms, not theirs. This ad would make it very hard for Republicans to dismiss my candidacy. I had voted to give Bush the authority to use force in Iraq, I had traveled to Iraq and Afghanistan many times, and I had publicly backed the Iraqi surge as early as 2005, when McCain proposed it. These were issues I had thought seriously about, and I knew I understood them better than any of my Republican opponents. I needed to exploit that fact politically. My viability depended on it.

"Let's make the ad," I said to Powell. "I'll stand up to Schumer and the DSCC if they resist us. He hasn't raised a penny for me yet, so he doesn't have much standing to dictate how I spend my money." The DSCC, in fact, early on considered Tennessee out of reach. Schumer hadn't built my campaign into his overall DSCC budget. Schumer was as tough and determined a Senate committee chair as the party had seen, and I respected him greatly for that, but he had not only ignored me and my campaign, he had also down talked loudly about me to national Democratic donors.

I decided to shoot the ad at the Baltimore port. I walked along the harbor, against a backdrop of cranes and container ships. "President Bush wants to sell this port and five others to the United Arab Emirates," I said, "a country that was home to two 9/11 hijackers, and had banks wire money to the terrorists. I'm running for the Senate because we should not outsource our national security to anyone. I'll fight to protect America and keep your family safe."

As we were filming the ad, Powell's cell phone rang. He listened and handed the phone to me. "It's Schumer," he said. "He's mad."

"He's still against it?" I asked. Powell nodded.

"Senator, how are you?" I said into the phone.

"Harold, this is not smart," Schumer said, characteristically dispensing with conventional phone etiquette. "You can't spend on TV this early in a campaign. Voters won't remember your message, and it's fewer dollars you'll have to spend at the end, when you actually need it."

"Senator, the campaign is starting to gain traction, and right now Tennessee voters are fixated on George Bush's decision to sell the management and control of our ports to a Middle Eastern country. I need to make clear where I stand on this issue. This ad will be a hit. It will be remembered at least long enough for me to make my next political point in the campaign. And I need to sustain my viability."

"Look, I agree that it may be a winning issue," Schumer said, "but you're wrong to think it will have an impact now. This is the wrong time to run this ad. I'm urging you not to do this."

"Chuck, I'm doing the ad," I said. The conversation did not end on a pleasant note.

The ad started running the next week, and it was a huge hit. Media outlets across Tennessee were talking about it. It got national attention—the major Sunday shows covered it and used the ad to demonstrate how Democrats could counter the Republican advantage on national security. And my fundraising picked up nationally. Many others started to criticize the administration. Even Republicans urged Bush to change course.

But the real kicker was watching Schumer on one of the cable news shows the following week commenting on the ad. He praised the ad, and he then praised me for having the courage to run it. He even told viewers that he'd encouraged me to do it! All I could think was—my man Chuck.

When I next saw him in D.C., he said, "Harold—nice job. Get out there and keep pushing and figure out how to win this thing." He smiled while he was saying it.

But Chuck and I would continue to have differences early in my campaign because he wouldn't let up on criticizing me to national donors. Even though I was picking up momentum in the state, Chuck thought I was spending too much too soon. I called and asked for a meeting at his DSCC office to ask him to stop hurting my campaign. It was one of the more memorable political meetings I've ever had. Chuck and I laugh about it now, but it was not a cordial encounter. Schumer, his deputy J. B. Poersch, Michael Powell, and I sat at a simple conference table. Schumer, who had come in fifteen minutes late, was at the head of the table. He was the boss, and he wanted me and everyone else to know it.

Schumer went right at me, saying that despite the success of my security ad, my spending was going to hurt me in the long run. I said,

> I disagree with you fully. Chuck, with all due respect, you know very little about my state. You know very little about Tennessee or my race. The DSCC hasn't executed a successful strategy to win in the South in a long time, and you certainly don't have a strategy for a black guy to win in the South. Let me run my race. Believe me, I want to win. I'm not interested in raising people's money to waste it, but the only way I can stay viable is to spend money early. I need to be in the game *now*. The odds are stacked

against me in the eyes of people around the country, and I have to show continued upward movement in the polls. I have to show some fight. This is a calculated, strategic choice.

I reminded him how much attention the Republican primary would draw in June and July 2006, right before the August primary. I would be shut out of the conversation, I argued:

I cannot have the entire political conversation in Tennessee revolve around the Republican primary. If I wait until after the Republican primary, the only names the public will know will be the three Republican candidates, with the winner being foremost in people's minds. Trying to get into the game that late makes no sense, and frankly, if I follow your strategy, Chuck, I won't raise as much because the poll numbers will continue to show me way down. I'm not going to put myself in the position of saying to people: I'm twenty points down, now please write me a check. Five points down in August is obviously an easier distance to cover. I have to be right there at the end to be able to raise another few million dollars down the stretch, and I have a funny feeling you and the DSCC won't help me if I'm down twenty in August. And I'm not going to allow that to happen, Chuck.

Schumer remained dismissive and kept pushing for a conventional approach. He wanted me to hug my money until the primary and come out swinging in August. I reminded him that being twenty down wasn't the way to start the general campaign. "I can't do that, Chuck."

I also reminded him that I hadn't asked for anything and the DSCC hadn't given me anything. "I'm not forfeiting anything here," I said. "When you rank your top ten races, I'm number eleven. At this point, all I'm asking you to do is not bad-mouth me to Democratic donors. If you choose not to be helpful, I understand. I would hope that you would choose otherwise. But I would ask that you not hurt me with donors."

Schumer didn't budge. He said, "You can't count on us spending money on you if you're going to spend recklessly now. We're going to need to make a lot of tough decisions about where to spend. We will consider your behavior now as we make decisions in the future."

I wanted to say, "F— you, Chuck." Instead, I said, "If I'm in a dead heat in this race in October two things will happen, Chuck. First, you will take credit for everything we've done, and then you will spend money on this race because we may make the difference in you winning a majority in the U.S. Senate." Schumer looked at me, staring—but I knew he agreed. He wouldn't say it, because he's CHUCK SCHUMER and always has to be right and get the last word.

"First you gotta get yourself into a dead heat," he said.

"If you stop telling people I was running a bad campaign, it would help," I said.

At this point, temperatures had risen and voices were raised. Finally, Michael Powell jumped in and said, "Hey, let's start over here, guys. We all want the same outcome. Let's figure out where we are. We want to make sure you guys have a sense of what we're doing strategically. Let's talk about how we're going to spend our money from here on out and how we can best work together."

We pushed the reset button. Schumer and the DSCC came around on me in an important way. We may have had our differences early on, but Chuck was a good ally at the end. And I was appreciative.

THE MAIN REASON we were gaining traction was because I was outworking my opponents. Every weekend Congress was out and each congressional break, I was canvassing the state with my driver, counselor, and friend, Matt Reel. Matt had previously worked for my colleague, Congressman Lincoln Davis. Lincoln loaned him to me. Matt became a friend. He and I crisscrossed the state every week. I spent more time with Matt than I did with anyone in the beginning of the campaign. Later we added Jon Davidson who also became a good friend. We started at five in the morning and ended at eleven or midnight. It was event after event after event and little city after little city after little city.

One of my big challenges was to convince voters that I could represent the whole state. People wondered whether someone from Memphis could understand the needs of the rest of the state—particularly the needs of rural Tennesseans. I needed to be familiar with the distinct sets of concerns prevailing in every part of the state.

So I went to every quadrant of the state. I made every kind of public event. I went to small-town parades and visited small businesses and schools. I met with pastors and school principals and sheriffs. I attended community celebrations all across the state. I'll never forget a big annual summer parade I went to in Kingsport, in northeastern Tennessee. One of the traditions of the parade is pelting the participants with water balloons. As I walked through the parade, I was pummeled with water balloons. I thought it was because they didn't like my politics, but at the end of the parade, the grand marshal looked at me and said, "Young man, you did well."

"What do you mean I did well?" I asked. "They water-ballooned the heck out of me."

"The more water balloons you get hit with," he said, "the more they like you. That's the tradition."

I stopped at every chain restaurant in the state: Cracker Barrel, O'Charley's, Outback Steakhouse, Golden Corral, Shoney's, Sizzler, Applebee's, and T.G.I. Friday's. And I ate at local meat-and-three-vegetable spots where I could find them.

If we were in a county in which I didn't know many people, I would tell Matt, "Pick the hottest restaurant in town. Let's get a big table and let me work the room." It wasn't always easy to put a rally together in some small counties, so I went wherever the people were—just as I had done in my first congressional race.

I'd start talking to one table, and talk just loud enough so that other people in the restaurant could hear me. I'd watch to see who was listening, and then I would go talk to them.

Occasionally, people were rude, but by and large people welcomed me. There was always someone who wanted to meet me and talk to me.

I believed, as I always had, that if I was able to talk to voters in person, I could win their support or, at a minimum, leave them with a positive impression of me. So no one was a stranger. Oftentimes, my strategy boiled down to listening. I remember visiting a Waffle House outside Nashville early on a summer morning. Matt was going to run in and get something to go, but there were four cars and a truck in the parking lot, three full tables of patrons, and one guy at the counter. I saw a chance to win over ten voters, so I jumped out of the car and went in. The customers, all men, had obviously just worked the night shift somewhere nearby. They weren't in a real talkative mood. But I had to figure out how to connect with them, just as I'd had to figure out how to connect with kindergartners and their parents during my first congressional campaign.

I walked up to each table, thanked the men for a hard night's work, and asked, "What's the one thing you wish government would do differently for the working man and his family?" The question engaged them. The most common answers I got—and this held true at many similar breakfast spots across the state—were "Lower my taxes and get off my back" and "Stop spending money we don't have to fight wars we can't win."

These impromptu listening sessions were as valuable as anything I did during the campaign. People expressed their concerns differently in different places, but their core concerns were the same: Government wasn't working like it should. I was a Blue Dog Democrat, which meant, among other things, that I was committed to making government live within its means. I understood.

The majority of Tennesseans wanted the same things out of government, and they were the things I had supported throughout my time in Congress. No one wanted to be over-taxed. Everyone wanted the nation safe and our troops and veterans taken care of. Every parent wanted a good education and a good job for his or her children. Every family wanted high-quality, affordable health insurance. Everyone worried that the government was spending too much money with too little to show for it. These planned and unplanned campaign stops helped crystallize what was arguably the most important and toughest task of the campaign: convincing voters that I understood what they wanted—and that I wanted the same. I was one of them.

Matt and I collected contact information wherever we went and from everyone we met. Early in the campaign, we were collecting 300 to 500 new contacts a week. That number increased to over 1,000 a week by the late summer of 2005. The information, which included e-mail addresses, would go into a database at my headquarters. Every evening, I would send out an e-mail to everyone in my database in which I sum-marized the day: what I had done, whom I had met, and what I had learned about Tennessee and the hopes of Tennesseans.

This started accidentally. Late one evening in June, we were driving from Murfreesboro to Nashville. We'd had a great night. I had listened to the husbands and wives of Na-tional Guard soldiers talking about how tough it was to raise a family after losing a breadwinning spouse to overseas deployment. These men and women were not angry or resentful, but they were quietly issuing a plea for help. I sent out an e-mail in which I said that I planned to introduce legislation that would grant employers a full tax deduction if they continued to pay part-time soldiers serving in Iraq or Afghanistan. I asked my supporters to pray for these families and their loved ones serving overseas.

The response I got about the e-mail was overwhelming. I wasn't trying to trigger this kind of response from the people in my database, but it hooked me, and I started sending out e-mails every evening. Soon, supporters in my database were forwarding my messages to their friends and families, and so on.

This correspondence gave people a sense of inclusion in and ownership of the campaign. I always mentioned people by name in my e-mails.

I'll never forget being at an event in a small town called Smithville, in middle Tennessee. A lady approached me and said excitedly, "Congressman Ford, I saw you were in my cousin's town!" Thinking my visit was covered on TV that evening, I said, "You saw it?" She said, "Yes, I got the e-mail. My cousin sent me a copy of the e-mail that had her name in it—she was so excited to see it."

People wrote to say that they were following me on the trail and planned to do it throughout the campaign. They wanted to know if I was really writing the e-mails myself. I wrote them all. Sometimes, I would miss a day or two, and people would immediately start asking about the lag: "Hey, I haven't gotten an e-mail the past two days. What's going on with the campaign?"

"I'm working on it," I would write. "I don't let anybody else write my e-mails, so sometimes it takes a little longer."

These e-mail interactions ended up helping to quell doubts about my candidacy, because they allowed me to confront the doubts and doubters head-on and in real time. Furthermore, writing the e-mails helped me to organize my arguments and keep perspective and track our progress—as slow as it was.

THE GOP CANDIDATES, Ed Bryant, Bob Corker, and Van Hilleary, dismissed me from the start, too. They didn't think an African American, let alone a Democrat named Ford, could win a Senate race in Tennessee. They believed my uncle's indictment would sink me. They hardly mentioned me early on in their hard-fought, intensively covered primary.

But I was determined to be a part of the conversation. I had to be. If I wasn't, the Republican nominee would stroll to victory that November.

I was unimpressed with my Republican opponents as strong campaigners and big thinkers. Ed and Van were former members of Congress. We all were friends. In fact, I liked them both, but neither of them struck me as a dynamic leader. In contrast, Corker was very proud of himself. He was wealthy and arrogant. He had received high marks as mayor of

Chattanooga, but the more we investigated Corker's record, the more it became apparent that his high impressions of himself weren't consistent with Chattanooga voters' attitudes toward him. I actually won more votes in Chattanooga than Corker did. A majority of the people who knew him best voted against him for Senate.

Neither Corker, Bryant, nor Hilleary wanted to engage me on an issue—not Iraq, not the economy, and certainly not the lack of fiscal responsibility coming out of Washington. I wanted to talk about all of these things. As well as education. And energy. And entitlements.

As primary day grew closer, it was becoming increasingly clear that Corker was going to win. Corker was spending millions of his own fortune to finance his campaign. The polls showed that it was paying off for him. My campaign slowly but surely started to focus on Corker.

I figured that Corker—like most rich guys who run for public office—would take a few weeks off after the primary. His team, I knew, believed that I was a lightweight. Corker thought the same. So while Corker took the first two and a half weeks of August off, I didn't. I stayed on the road working, visiting farms, fairs, and high school football practices. I wanted to establish something early—the pace of the campaign. I knew Corker was lazy; meaning, he wouldn't work as hard as I was. And I wanted to show Corker and the state that I welcomed debates. I knew that Corker didn't want to debate me.

He was not a great debater. Not only did Corker not have a firm grasp of the issues, his standard response to questions he didn't have a thoughtful answer to was "I'm from Tennessee, and I'm gonna do things the Tennessee way."

He eventually agreed to three debates—one was on a Saturday night while UT played Georgia in football. Whenever he used the "Tennessee way" line, I would look at him and say, "Mr. Corker, that's not the Tennessee way. The Tennessee way is to create jobs. The Tennessee way is to keep America safe. The Tennessee way is to help bring our Tennessee National Guard members home—many are now on their third and fourth tours in Iraq—and to end this war in a smart, responsible way. That's the Tennessee way."

But Corker was trying to highlight something other than the Tennessee way—he was subtly telling voters that a five-term congressman from Memphis wasn't their kind of Tennessee. So I had to be equally aggressive. Anytime he launched an attack, we answered it immediately—if we hadn't already preempted it—and with more force. When he accused me of being weak on security, for example, I responded harder. As mayor of Chattanooga, Corker had cut the pay of police officers and firefighters while raising his own mayoral salary. I said in a campaign ad, "He's a millionaire who raised his own salary while cutting pay for our first responders. Is this the kind of leadership we want in Washington?" I organized a press conference in Chattanooga with the local police, and asked again, "Why would you cut their pay, Mr. Corker? You may have a good reason. We would just like to know what it is."

Every type of attack I had predicted materialized. Corker claimed that I voted for abortion for underage girls, which I hadn't. He ran an ad in which a cartoon character of me walks into the Capitol and votes for gay marriage, which I had not. Often when I entered campaign events, I was greeted by anti-choice fanatics holding baby dolls with smashed-in heads. "Baby killer, baby killer, baby killer!" they would scream at me. All I could think as I walked by them time after time was "How can we as Democrats allow these extremists to own the political language of 'life'?"

After about the fifteenth event in which these "life" extremists protested outside, I decided to take a different approach with them. I invited the extremists into my events if they promised to be civil and respectful (they often failed that test and had to be escorted out). While they sat in the audience, I would remind everyone that the anti-choice protesters claimed to be pro-life, but not one of them protested when newborns were denied free health care and affordable early childhood education initiatives. I would continue, "Not one of you protesters differed with or hurled profanity at Donald Rumsfeld when he told some of Tennessee's bravest war fighters that they should go to war with the equipment they had and not the equipment they wanted and needed. Not one of these extremists cares enough about or appreciates comprehensively the meaning of life. I refuse to allow you to call yourself pro-life. In fact, those of us in favor of increased education and health care spending on kids and increased spending for veterans and soldiers on the battlefield are the real pro-lifers."

I was always met with loud applause from my supporters and loud protests from the anti-choicers. I would routinely lead my supporters in the chant, "We're pro-life."

◆　　　◆

I RAN ADS countering Corker's attacks. I went on the offensive with an ad that showed me in my church defending myself against Corker's and the Republican Party's vicious and false character attacks. I knew it would get lots of attention.

Powell wrote the ad. And the message was straightforward—that I am a man of faith who was taught the difference between right and wrong at home and then in church, and who is not afraid to promote his faith. The ad was the biggest and most important statement I made during the general campaign. It put Corker and the RNC back on their heels. The ad was so effective that both Corker and the RNC used parts of it in their attack ads in response. The RNC and the Tennessee Republican Party even instigated an IRS investigation into whether federal tax laws were violated by my church giving me permission to film an ad in the sanctuary. The inquiry was eventually dropped and found to be without merit. It had political merit but not legal merit.

My church ad helped us surge. Public polls heading into late September showed me gaining—a *USA Today* poll showed me with a small lead, inside the margin of error. You could feel momentum shifting my way. I remember one of my senior campaign advisers and friends, Tom Lee, telling me that many of his Republican friends were warming up to me. They liked my moderate to conservative approach to solving problems. They liked the fact that I was committed to balanced budgets and that I was pro-business. In short, I was their kind of Democrat. My chief of staff, Bobby Sepucha, believed we were overcoming my uncle's legal troubles. Even though I'd made several mistakes along the way—including confronting Corker at a private airport hangar in Memphis and appearing at a fund-raiser for a Tennessee Democratic state senate candidate who had openly embraced an income tax for Tennesseans as the remedy to the state's fiscal woes—I had proven to voters that I could be trusted to represent them in Washington. If there were two things I could have taken back during the campaign, it would be those two actions. I had worked so hard to establish credibility and maturity. Those actions hurt me but they weren't fatal. Corker needed more. He was becoming more and more desperate because of the tight polls.

IN 2006, TENNESSEE was the only state with a competitive Senate race where President Bush's approval ratings didn't drop below 50 percent at any point in the race. In fact, Bush never dropped below 52 percent—a fact that proved very helpful to Corker. Bush visited Tennessee a half-dozen times during my race. But Corker and the Republicans worried because my numbers weren't dropping and the election was fewer than twenty-five days away. Corker brought in a new campaign manager at the behest of the RNC. Both Bill Frist and Lamar Alexander ratcheted up their language toward me. Lamar regularly traveled to heavily Republican areas in northeast Tennessee and routinely offered, "We don't need a Memphis congressman representing us in the U.S. Senate." *A Memphis congressman.* We got the word that Corker's desperation had triggered a reversal in strategy. They were going to launch an all-out assault with race being the organizing and consistent theme.

My finance chairman, Charles Robert Bone, got a call from a good friend, the former chair of the Tennessee Republican Party, who knew Corker's senior campaign team. He had actually told us weeks earlier that the Republicans would play clean—no race stuff, he meant.

"Remember when I told you I thought the Corker campaign wouldn't get too ugly?" he reminded Charles. "That they'd walk up to the line but not cross it? Well, they're not just going to cross it, they're going to step way over it. All bets are off. They're coming at him with everything they have. They're going nuclear."

It was around this time that a reporter from the *Washington Post* flew down to follow me for a day. She couldn't believe the way people were responding to me and the size of the crowds I was getting.

As we walked through one small town outside Chattanooga, she said to me, "Many of these people tell me they never voted for a Democrat, but they love you. They absolutely believe that you think differently, that you're a different kind of Democrat, and that you're going to bring change to Tennessee and to Washington. How did you convince them?"

I said,

We've been on the road working our tails off for two years. I've been here fifteen times. I stop in town whenever I come through. In towns like this, people remember you. If I have a piece of pound cake with someone, every-body will know what we talked about while we were eating it. I'm not coming just once to exchange a few handshakes for votes. I'm listening. I'm paying attention. That's why I have this kind of crowd. That's why people are starting to believe in me.

As we walked into the next event in the same town, I could hear the reporter asking an elderly white guy why he was supporting me.

He answered, "I believe in him. I believe what he's saying. I think he's going to go up to Washington and do a good job for us." He continued, "We need a change up there, and this guy, he's one of us. He's come here over and over, telling us what he's going to do. I believe he'll do it."

"You're really going to vote for him for Senate?" the reporter asked again, just to be sure she had heard it right the first time.

"Yeah," he said. "Look, it's not like he's dating my daughter. He just wants to be my senator."

She reported what the man said. Less than a week later, Corker and the RNC produced the now infamous "Call Me" ad, which featured a white, blonde actress wearing very little, claiming that she met me at a Playboy party. The ad ended with the same model looking into the camera and saying in a seductive voice, "Harold, call me." It was a powerful ad.

The first time I saw it all I could think was "This is brilliant." I told Powell that I wasn't going to go on TV and call the ad racist. That was what the Corker campaign hoped I would do. It would be the lead story on every network, and it risked alienating voters.

But I had to condemn the indecency of the ad. I called it repulsive and said that Corker and the RNC should be ashamed of themselves for forcing Tennessee families to watch half-naked women on TV lie about a political candidate. The Republicans had been trying to highlight throughout the campaign this Playboy party rumor but couldn't verify it. They also wanted to highlight that I dated white women. The ad hit at my dating habits and reminded people I was black.

Corker's people had been searching and searching for info on the Playboy mansion. Reporters would ask me if I had been to the Playboy mansion in Los Angeles. I had—and have—never been to the Playboy mansion. The Republicans were confused. Finally, a reporter got the question right in Nashville.

"Did you go to a party sponsored by *Playboy* after the Super Bowl last year?" she asked.

I said, "I did. It was a party hosted by *Playboy* and some other companies. I believe I went for about an hour, along with about 2,500 other people."

She asked, "Why did you go?"

I said, "Well, I like girls. I like football. And it was after the Super Bowl."

Afterward, Mike Powell looked at me and laughed nervously. "We'll see what happens," he said.

The press coverage focused on my "I like girls and I like

football" line. Some people thought it was funny—it was football season, and every guy in the state understood what I was saying. Some, especially Corker and the RNC, saw it as an opportunity to make up some ground in the polls. The ad started soon thereafter.

Corker quickly denounced the RNC and the ad and tried to distance himself and his campaign from it. The ad was paid for by the RNC, which was chaired by Ken Mehlman. Mehlman publicly defended the ad, saying that it was not racist. But Corker's distancing from the ad confirmed that it was at a minimum inappropriate and offensive. Further, Corker's denouncing of the ad was dishonest. Corker traveled with the senior RNC official on the ground in Tennessee every day and all day. When he issued his denial, she was standing right behind him, which prompted my campaign spokesman, Tom Lee, to say, "Mr. Corker is acting surprised and upset, but instead of complaining to the press now, why didn't he just ask the RNC official who travels with him as part of his campaign team not to run the ad in the first place if he's so offended?"

Corker and I both knew that he needed and benefited from the ad—the polls confirmed it. He moved ahead of me. It was a turning point. And it didn't stop with the "Call Me" ad. That ad was one of three Corker ads that played on race. His radio ads were even worse. Indeed, the gloves had come off.

MONTHS BEFORE THESE Corker attack ads aired, I had planned a response in the event that the Republicans had decided to use race. My response was an ad featuring a former Tennessee Democratic governor, Ned McWherter, Tennessee's current Democratic governor, Phil Bredesen, and me. I had written the script in early 2006.

The three of us would be sitting in a barn, on stools, dressed in jeans and button-down shirts. First, Bredesen would make the case that I was committed to low taxes, balanced budgets, and pro-business conditions. "We have a candidate here who understands Tennessee," he would say. "Harold Ford understands our values. He understands that in Tennessee, we don't spend what we don't have, and we don't take what we don't need from taxpayers. Tennessee deserves better than what we're getting in D.C."

Then McWherter, who was the elder statesman in the Tennessee Democratic Party, would say, "I've known this boy all his life. I watched him grow up. He's always been his own thinker, his own man. He's gonna make each and every one of us proud to call him Senator Ford." McWherter spoke with a deep Tennessee drawl. He was the best and most credible force in Tennessee to validate me among rural voters. I wanted him to end the ad by looking over at me, grabbing my knee, and saying, "Harold, I already told them, you're all right."

Many people in Tennessee had never voted for anyone like me. I believed McWherter and Bredesen together could have answered the "Call Me" ad as well as the other RNC/Corker ads. Bredesen agreed to do it. But McWherter wouldn't. I really believe the ad would have made a big difference. Bredesen did other ads alone, which I appreciated. McWherter campaigned for me, but didn't do the ad.

We needed a plan B. Without McWherter, I got desperate for a moment and considered doing an anti-immigration ad. We had documents showing that Corker had hired illegal immigrants for construction projects and had been fined for it by the INS. Immigration was a big issue in the race, and when the question was posed to Corker during the course of the campaign, he publicly denied hiring illegal workers.

We could have used the documents to make a fairly devastating attack ad. Your mind goes to unwholesome places when your opponent abandons all morality. We imagined a voice-over like, "Bob Corker wants the INS to allow construction firms to hire illegal immigrants—because he did. That's how he made his money. And then he lied about it." We would have had forbidding images of illegal immigrants crossing a river or climbing a fence en masse, and we would have juxtaposed Corker's denial with the documents illustrating what he had done.

The decision not to do the anti-immigration ad was mine. It didn't feel right. It wasn't me. It would have been explosive. My politics couldn't sink to that level. As little as I thought of Corker and the Republicans for doing the "Call Me" ad, I refused to go there with them. Sometimes I wonder whether the anti-immigration ad would have altered the election's outcome.

The DSCC was running ads on my behalf. Unlike Corker and the RNC, I didn't work with the DSCC on their ads, and I didn't travel with a DSCC staffer. The DSCC ads were good, but they didn't have the impact at the end of the campaign that the RNC ads did.

By default, plan B ended up being more hard work. "Let's get back on the plane and outwork him," I said. So every day we woke up in northeastern Tennessee, in the eastern time zone, and we worked our way west to the state line in the central time zone. At around one in the morning, we'd get on the plane and fly back east, sleeping on the way. We'd land at 3:30 or 4:00 A.M., sleep for an hour and a half, and hit the early-morning radio shows and breakfast stops—all the while getting local press. Then we'd begin driving from town to town in the area, then fly to middle Tennessee. We'd land and make a stop at a lunch spot and a small business, getting press there, too. Then we'd get back on the plane in the late afternoon, fly 175 miles to west Tennessee, and repeat what we'd done in middle and east Tennessee. We did this for the final nine days of the campaign.

The Corker campaign assumed we would just fold in the face of their assault, but that final push got us back in the race. We were doing tracking polls every day, and we were gaining. We had dropped by ten points after the Playboy ad, and we got back to within one to two in the final three days. Our new approach helped close the gap.

Then on the Sunday before the election, the Memphis *Commercial Appeal* released findings of a poll showing me twelve points behind. They ran the story on the front page with an enormous headline. I didn't believe the numbers—I actually thought I had pulled ahead. You could feel the momentum moving toward us. The results of this poll ran in the

Memphis and Chattanooga newspapers on their front pages. It didn't deter me. But some observers believed we were going to lose. I'll never forget getting a call from Charlie Cook on the morning of Election Day. Charlie writes the *Cook Political Report*, which is the preeminent political journal on congressional and Senatorial races. He's the most sought-after predictor of Senate and House races in the country, and a friend.

"Harold," Charlie said,

I'm here looking at all this data, and you've run a hell of a race. I have no idea how you stayed in this race after what they did to you. It was an incredible campaign, but our numbers show that you're going to lose, and you're probably going to lose by less than three points. Unless something crazy happens today, I don't know how you overcome that. But whatever the outcome, give a great speech tonight, because you've given everything that you could to try to win against tall odds. You have a long future in this game. Be positive tonight, not negative. Your time will come again.

"I think I'm going to win," I said.

"I hope you do," he said. "But whatever happens, just realize that you will live to fight another day."

"I got you," I said.

I deeply appreciated his call. But I was planning to win.

◆　　　◆

BECAUSE THE CAMPAIGN had been so invigorated by that spontaneous visit to the Lil' Rebel a year earlier, I decided to make the Lil' Rebel my last official stop. The campaign bus pulled up to the bar late Monday afternoon. A large crowd, including local, national, and international press, had gathered outside. As soon as I got off the bus, the questions erupted: "Has the Playboy ad hurt you?" "Will race determine the outcome of this election?" "Are you going to make history tomorrow?" "How does it feel to be where it all started?"

"This has been a great race," I said, ignoring the questions. "And I want to thank the voters on this last day of campaigning for listening to me, challenging me, lifting me up—and putting up with me." The audience chuckled. "Most of all," I continued, "I want to thank you for giving me the chance to understand how I can give meaning and life to your aspirations as your senator in Washington."

The Lil' Rebel could hold thirty people uncomfortably, but there must have been seventy-five people crammed into the place when I walked in. Many of my friends were sitting at the bar, enjoying a late-afternoon beer after work.

I was in a great mood. I had given everything I had to the campaign. Despite some mistakes, I had no regrets, and I had thousands of new friends. I relished the back-and-forth with voters as much as I ever had. My two-year journey to win the hearts and minds of Tennesseans had reminded me over and over that politics was about helping people build better lives and futures, and my appetite for it remained undiminished.

A friend and former colleague from Congress, Joe Scarborough, had arranged to do a live segment at the Lil' Rebel for his then show *Scarborough Country*. Joe and I had worked together in Congress, collaborating on education and health legislation. When Joe's camera crew finished setting up, the place quieted down and we began the interview.

"You know, Joe," I told him, "I made my first visit to the Lil' Rebel"—there were loud cheers at the mention of the name—"at the very beginning of this campaign, and the people here showed me that all things were possible if I was willing to work hard, not be afraid to take the campaign to all corners of the state, and ask everyone for their support. The Lil' Rebel and its customers demonstrated to all who didn't believe that this campaign of ours, which started twenty-five points behind, could gain momentum and support throughout Tennessee."

"Well, Harold," Joe said, "you seem to be giving them a run for their money down there. It's hard to say whether you're going to win, but you should know that I'm for you. It may get me in trouble with my fellow Republicans, but I hope you win tomorrow. It would be good for Tennessee, the country, and the U.S. Senate. Good luck, friend."

After we left, I couldn't help reflecting on the campaign. I remembered my uncle's indictment the day after I announced, in late May of 2005. I recalled how many of my supporters and close advisers had told me that my campaign could never survive such a blow. I remembered fighting to convince Chuck Schumer and the DSCC that my credibility as a candidate depended on running TV ads early. And I remembered running into John, the Lil' Rebel regular, at a campaign event, and listening as he told me that the only way I could win was by stopping at every place like the Lil' Rebel I passed and by listening to every voter in Tennessee. Riding back to Memphis for the last time before the election, I felt good about how we ran this campaign.

GIVING THANKS

O N ELECTION NIGHT, I WATCHED THE RETURNS AT home with Emily, my then girlfriend, now wife. The campaign had rented rooms at the Peabody hotel, but I wanted to be at home alone to watch the initial returns.

Early vote returns from around the state started to flow in. I was beating Corker in Chattanooga. I was surprised and encouraged by that. I ended up winning Chattanooga by a few hundred votes.

After the race, Corker's campaign manager admitted to being shocked by the Chattanooga numbers. But as more and more numbers came in, I knew I couldn't make up the difference, even with a huge win in Memphis, which I got. Nashville had been sending its numbers in late because of voting machine irregularities. People there were fired up to vote for me, and they stood in line for hours—until 10:00 P.M. But even with these outstanding votes, there was no way I could make up the deficit. There just weren't enough votes left. It was too late now.

All I remember thinking was "It's over." I was numb. Emily

was crying. I said, "Don't cry, baby. I'm fine, and we'll do this again and win."

I went upstairs, took a shower, and got ready to go to the Peabody.

When we got to the Peabody ballroom, everyone was hugging and crying. I put my game face on and stayed positive. I had not written a concession speech. I hadn't written a victory speech either. I phoned Corker. "I just saw the numbers, Bob," I said. "Congratulations." Corker was cocky. I said, "Bob, good luck to you, bless you and your family, and take care," and I hung up the phone.

I took the stage shortly after the call. The place was packed. I saw friends and supporters who had flown in from everywhere—people I had known for twenty years and new friends who had offered financial support and believed in me right from the very beginning of the Senate race.

I looked at them, and it was painful. It was hard not to feel as if I had let every single one of them down. I thanked them all, and I thanked the voters of Tennessee, who had honored me by sharing their concerns and aspirations and who had listened to me in turn. And I thanked the voters of Memphis for electing me ten years earlier.

> These are moments you can either shrink from or grow from, and I'm going to ask my good Lord and Savior to give me the strength and wisdom and ability to grow and to not only be a better person, but to be a better servant.
>
> I say to my opponent tonight, congratulations to you and your family. I love my country more than I love this

process. And as debasing and demeaning as this process can be, we sometimes forget that when politics works, we live better lives and safer lives. When America is strong, the world is a better and safer place. I hope that my friends and colleagues in the Congress and the Senate understand what I learned in two years of campaigning: There is a hunger and a great appetite on the part of the American people for something much greater, and far more dignified, than what we've given them over the last several years. I say to everybody here: Don't lose faith in this great thing called America.

It's so easy, when these things happen, to get angry, and I hope that all of you who watched all this stuff during the campaign won't get angry about it. I'm reminded of my favorite piece of Scripture, quoted throughout this campaign, from the book of Ephesians: "For we wrestle not against flesh and blood, but against principalities and powers." And although we didn't get enough votes tonight, that Scripture holds just as true now as it did yesterday. And, Lord, I thank you for guiding and leading me, and ask that you continue to touch me and instruct me, and everybody here. Thank you, thank you, thank you, and God bless you.

I didn't stay around long afterward. I went backstage, shook a few hands, and headed upstairs with Emily to a suite in the hotel to try to get some sleep.

◆　　　◆

SHORTLY BEFORE GOING to bed, I got a call from President Clinton and Senator Hillary Clinton, and they couldn't have been more generous. They congratulated me for running a strong and positive race and nearly winning despite long odds. I thanked them for believing in me early, when I was down by more than twenty points. Then the former president of the United States gave me some advice:

> Harold, your future in politics will be determined more by how you behave tomorrow morning than by anything else you do after this race. Remember, I lost two races, so I know how it feels. But you need to get up in the morning, without being angry, and travel around Tennessee thanking the voters, as if you had won the race. In a lot of ways, you've been humbled by the voters, and they're testing you. You have to prove that you meant what you campaigned on—and that was a love of country and politics and a desire to make life better through the political system. What the Republicans did to you was despicable, and they will have to answer for that, but in the meantime, don't let their disgraceful ways define you before the voters.

Senator Clinton took the phone from the president and, in a very warm, motherly way, said she was proud of the race I had run. "And I'm not convinced," she added, "that you've lost this race. I know you've conceded already, but I must tell you I don't put it past the Republicans to try to steal this race from you after the kind of campaign they ran."

"I hear you, Senator," I said, "and I thank you, but we've done the math and we can't close the margin. It amounts to about 25,000 votes. I want to thank you for all you and the president did for me and my family in the race. I won't forget it. I'm with Emily, and she says hello and thank you, too. I look forward to helping you in the future. Please give the president my thanks again. We love you, and God bless."

THE NEXT MORNING, I got up early and began making thank-you telephone calls to my supporters across the state. Most were still sleeping, so I ended up leaving a lot of messages. One of my best friends, Mike Eisner, knocked on the door. "I know you need a Starbucks," he said, "so let's go get one." We had a long day ahead of us.

I had decided to take President Clinton's advice and stick to my postcampaign travel schedule. Matt Reel and Mike Powell had held the private plane we'd chartered a few days before, thinking we would be traveling to different parts of the state to thank voters for a victory. I had lost, but I still owed the more than 850,000 people who had voted for me a thank-you.

For the next two days, I was in motion. I went to Tri-Cities, Chattanooga, Knoxville, and Nashville. I went to little towns where I had done well and to little towns where I had not done well.

People were unfailingly supportive. They often broke into applause when I arrived. They were appreciative, and sometimes surprised, that I had come. Emotions were still raw. There were hugs, tears, and words of encouragement. There were expressions of gratitude and outrage ("I can't believe they ran those ads!" was a comment I heard more than once).

I was profoundly disappointed, but I wasn't angry, dejected, or bitter, and I wanted people to know that. "To my supporters in the community," I said, "thank you for being there for me. Thank you for two years of believing in me and believing in this campaign. I'm sorry I let you down. To the other voters in the community, thank you for giving me a hearing."

I'll never forget stopping at a diner in a small town where I'd gotten maybe 35 percent of the vote. I introduced myself and said, "I want to thank you for giving me a chance to come visit during the campaign. You listened to me. You may not have voted for me, but you spent time with me and allowed me to get to know you. I will always be grateful for that, and I hope you give me the chance to come back again."

After I had finished speaking, a man came up to me and said, "This is unbelievable. You came by and I shook your hand, but I didn't vote for you. And now you come back still to thank me. Hell, the guy I voted for hasn't come here yet!" He grabbed my hand. "I won't forget it. Safe travels home, Ford. See you again."

I have never forgotten that conversation, or the many similar ones I had during my thank-you tour. Revisiting the paths of the campaign brought me closure and allowed me to move on. It reminded me that I still loved politics and the hope that it promised.

AFTERWORD

FOR THE MOMENT, MY ELECTED POLITICAL LIFE HAD ended, but I was determined to remain a part of the national political conversation and to stay involved in policymaking. Right away, I was offered the chairmanship of the Democratic Leadership Council (DLC), which I was grateful to accept. In Congress, I had worked with the DLC on school reform, trade, and budget matters. DLC founder and friend Al From had traveled with me to Tennessee to promote charter schools.

In addition, I accepted a teaching position at Vanderbilt University in the political science department. I signed on as a commentator for Fox News, which gave me a large media platform to discuss and engage in policy debates. I made good friends at Fox, including Roger Ailes, Shepard Smith, Sean Hannity, and Alan Colmes. A year later, I moved to NBC/MSNBC, where I am now.

But I wanted more than a continuing presence in the political arena. I wanted private-sector experience as well. I had been in public service all my life. After the Senate race, several large corporations expressed interest in me and eventually offered me positions.

One of my mentors, Richard Holbrooke, gave me terrific advice on how to balance my appetite for public policy with the need to make a living. I went to see my friends Greg Fleming and Jason Wright at Merrill Lynch, who introduced me to CEO Stan O'Neal. I eventually decided on Merrill. Having Greg and Jason there made it the right fit.

As a Merrill Lynch vice chairman, I met with the CEOs and board members of corporations spanning multiple sectors—tech, financial services, health, and energy—and worked alongside Merrill partners to maintain and broaden our relationships with banking clients. It was fascinating to me how political and policy developments in Washington affected investor behavior, the movement of capital, the valuations of companies, and the prospects for economic growth.

ALTHOUGH TENNESSEE REMAINED home for more than two years after my Senate race, spending time in New York brought me and Emily closer. Emily had lived in New York City since graduating from the University in Miami in 2003. She worked as a marketing executive for Carolina Herrera and Nina Ricci. She had made New York her home. It would eventually become our home.

An investment banker and close friend of mine named Alan

Garner, who is originally from Memphis, introduced us to First Presbyterian Church, at Twelfth Street and Fifth Avenue. Emily and I both liked and admired the pastor, Jon Walton, and we began attending regularly. We both felt at home at First Presbyterian. Plus, it's only six blocks from where we live.

As time went on, I was enjoying New York more and more. I was spending two to three days a week in the city. I was on the road more than I was anywhere, though. I proposed to Emily in October 2007 and we married that next April. I still believed that Emily and I would move back to Tennessee permanently, because I was seriously considering running for governor in 2010.

"You're going to have a hard time explaining your New York happiness back in Tennessee," my friend Joe Scarborough told me one morning after *Morning Joe*. Joe was right. After the 2008 presidential race, I decided that New York was going to be my home because I was getting increasingly involved in New York life—philanthropic, commercial, and political. I announced in early 2009 that I wasn't going to run for governor of Tennessee.

Tennessee was where I was born, but New York was where I wanted to make my life with my wife and the family we want to start. The energy, dynamism, and spirit of New York fit me more than any other place I had ever lived or spent time in. In fact, New York City renewed my spirit and energy. Starting a political life wasn't my motivation at all. However, I quickly realized that moving from Tennessee to New York didn't mean I had to abandon my political interests and aspirations.

"New York will fully embrace you," a New York friend told me just after I made my decision to move to New York. "As soon as you fully embrace it."

AND I HAVE.

Acknowledgments

So many people helped make this book a reality, but I have to thank Sean Desmond, Jeff Tietz, Richard Abate, Matt Johnson, and Rick Rosen for believing in and having patience with me and my story. The book wouldn't have happened without each of you, especially Jeff and Sean.

I want to thank everyone who worked in the congressional office with me on behalf of the constituents of the Ninth District of Tennessee, especially Mark Schuermann, David Sutphen, Marland Buckner, Amy Mollenkamp, Nichole Francis, Bobby Sepucha, Scott Keefer, Clay Perry, Tracey Goodman, Jarvis Stewart, Maura Black, Sharonda Brown, Ellen Chube, Sherman Greer, Jerry Fanion, Kim Herndon, Jessica Elledge, John Freeman, Robert White, and Teal Baker. The work each of you did made lives better for people who wanted nothing more than to be treated fairly and with dignity. We tried our best. A very special thanks goes to Mark Schuermann, Bobby Sepucha, and Sherman Greer for helping with research on the book. Couldn't have finished the book without the three of you.

I also want to thank my friends Brian and Lavinia Snyder, Dylan Glenn, Erik Gordon, Jason, Sarah, and Rachel Hohenberg, Uncle Eddie, Bren Simon, Dick Beattie, Dale, Julie, and Jack Allen, Chad Brownstein, Mike Eisner, Hassan and Amy

Murphy, Alfred Liggins, Richard and Lisa Plepler, Raul and Jean Marie Fernandez, Todd Bradley, Ron Blaylock, and Amy Hayes for the love and support they showed me and my wife during the writing of this book.

I want to thank Claudia Weaver, John Geer, Tom Lee, Carol Andrews, and Elizabeth Lowery for helping and working to make this book happen.

Finally, I want to thank Anne Finucane, Andrea Smith, and the entire Bank of America Merrill Lynch team.

And last, I love you Em, Mom, Dad, Jake, Isaac, Andrew, Ava, Michelle, Source, Tommy, Anson, Maria, TJ, Leslie, Jonathan, and Vin.

Go Blue!

About the Author

HAROLD FORD, JR., is an executive vice chairman at Bank of America in New York. In addition, he teaches public policy at New York University's Wagner Graduate School of Public Service and chairs the Democratic Leadership Council. He and his wife, Emily, live in Manhattan.